To Stand
Hope,
           Jerry
           11/28/2020

Jay's book is filled front to back with practical ideas on how to - and how not to - treat women. A must-read for every single guy over 50! --Rob C. (Florida)

Easy read; great stories and to the point! I strongly recommend! --Lucian M. (Colorado)

I enjoyed the book; easy to read. I recommend it. --Bruce M. (Connecticut)

Your book seems to be a cross section of personal experiences tying in with reflections from them...enabling you to choose a different attitude towards relationships in general! Great strategies...partnered with nurturing empathies, make a cool hand Luke approach to the men of our age who are looking for guidance and direction!!! Well done. --Michael D. and Jude G., (Queensland Australia)

I enjoyed reading this book and customers coming to my beauty shop (men & women) also enjoyed it. We have fun discussing the different stories. --Judy M., (New York)

This is a great guidebook for those BB men looking for BB women. It is a fun read and very informative. Men will find this book very helpful. --Kathy & Alan H. (New York)

I have enjoyed reading your book, it's well written, right to the point and certainly with a great sense of humor. You know us baby boomer ladies well! --Ursula L. (California)

After reading this book, many women will chuckle and say, "I know a guy just like the one described in the book!"

Bewildered, many guys will answer, "Who Me?"

Baby Boomer Women

How To Form a Lasting Relationship With Them

Jay Ferry

Baby Boomer Women by Jay Ferry
Published by CreateSpace Independent Publishing Platform

SECOND EDITION; updated and expanded October 2017.

For questions or for more information contact the author at: JayFerryauthor@yahoo.com

All rights reserved. No part of this publication may be reproduced, stored in a retrieval system, or transmitted in any form or by any means – electronic, mechanical, photocopy, recording, or any other – except for brief quotations in printed reviews, without the prior written permission of the author.

Copyright © 2017 by Jay Ferry
All rights reserved.

International Standard Book Numbers:
ISBN-13: 978-1547276875
ISBN-10: 1547276878

Printed in the United States of America

DEDICATION

This book is dedicated to the 58,600 brothers who gave the ultimate sacrifice in Vietnam and the additional 175,000 who committed suicide afterward because of mental scars from serving in that war.

They were robbed of their chance to have the pleasure of aging with and loving the most wonderful generation of women...

The Baby Boomer Women.

I also am deeply indebted to my superhuman mom Elsie, my breathtaking wife Lori, my remarkable daughter Nicole, my incredible lady Ali, my grandchildren Ella, Guy, and Vivian, my loving grandmother Anna, and the many special women and dance partners whom I have the great pleasure in knowing, I humbly thank you for "Having more faith in me than a beach has sand."

CONTENTS

INTRODUCTION 1
1 Baby Boomers: Who Are They? 4
2 Assess Yourself... Who Is the Real You? 12
3 Before Meeting Them 26
4 Where to Meet Them 42
5 That First Introduction 74
6 Communication and Conversations 82
7 The First Date: Do's and Don'ts 96
8 Moving Forward 115
9 Keep it Rolling? 123
10 And Away We Go... 130
Appendix I Great Easy Recipes 134
About the Author 154

INTRODUCTION

Here he was, thinking that last night's date went well and that she'd return his text today.

Alas, no return communication.

This has happened so many times. I always seem to do well on the first date, yet I can't ever seem to be able to get a second date.

What am I doing wrong?

I had originally thought of a catchy title such as *A Dummy's Guide to Dating Baby Boomer Women*. However, parts if it can also pertain to BB women seeking a meaningful relationship with a BB man. Still, the main audience for this book is BB men seeking BB women. Some of it can also be applied to how BB women can mold a meaningful relationship with a BB man by filtering out some of BB man's crudeness in language, manners, dress, and actions. Some of the items in his book can also be applied to dating in general.

I am not a psychologist or sociologist, nor have I ever worked for any kind of dating or matchmaking service. I am merely an observer of people's actions and mannerisms and I have seen some very successful ways in which BBs have formed wonderful relationships. I have listened to many BB women who have relayed great romance stories. I have also heard many women tell stories of absolute disasters in dating.

I have witnessed firsthand men doing things that result in absolute disasters with regard to having a chance at compatibility and happiness with BB women. So although I do not claim to be an expert in this area, I am sure that if you follow my suggestions and advice, you will have a better chance of meeting, dating, and forming a wonderful, lasting relationship with a BB woman.

BABY BOOMER WOMEN

This book is mainly about American baby boomers. Naturally, cultural differences shaped the boomers in the USA that were unique to this country. Some of those differences with people of other countries were sufficiently drastic that most of this book applies to Americans. However, there are some general guidelines that can be followed regardless of the person's country of origin.

Most of us baby boomers have been married and, for one reason or another, are now single. If you think about it honestly, you might agree that life is just better when you have someone with whom to share it. Seeing and experiencing the greatness of our world is simply not as much fun when you are doing it alone. Wasn't seeing Yosemite, the Grand Canyon, or Crater Lake for the first time more awesome when you were with someone else to see it, understand it, and appreciate it?

Many of us boomers are retired and are now in the travel mode. Remember when Dinah Shore used to sing "See the USA in your Chevrolet?" With more affordable airfares or getting buddy passes from our children, the world is now much smaller. Jetting away to Europe, Hawaii, or the Orient has become much more commonplace.

With the adventure and convenience of recreational vehicles, the wonders of America and Canada are just outside our mobile bedrooms. America has 59 national parks! How many have you visited?

There are wonders like Yellowstone, the Great Smoky Mountains, and Denali to name just a few. Canada offers Prince Edward Island, Banff, the Canadian Rockies, and many more. If you're a city person you might want to explore the great cities of Toronto, Quebec City, Vancouver, San Diego, Chicago, and Orlando. They are all literally at our doorstep.

So throw away the remote, erase network TV dribble, and forget about the overpaid professional athletes. Get out and

Introduction

enjoy life with a classy BB woman! Follow the basic ideas in this book and you should be able to find the best woman to enjoy life with as a couple instead of as an individual.

Remember, this book is not only for BB men. It could also be a gift from a BB woman to a BB man. If you're receiving this book as a gift, someone cares about you! Read it and watch it guide you into a better and more loving relationship.

I have included numerous stories to illustrate the concepts being discussed. Although the stories are real, I have changed all names to allow for privacy. Any perceived similarities to actual people are purely coincidental.

Okay, let's get started! If you keep these four concepts in mind, you're off to a great start!

Grooming = Impeccable Personal Hygiene

Manners = Respect

Loyalty = Truthfulness

Integrity = Character

1
Baby Boomers: Who Are They?

Much has been written and discussed about what the counselors call the Four C's of a successful relationship: Chemistry, Communication, Compatibility, and Commitment.

    The concept behind these qualifications is good. The degree by which these qualities control a successful relationship changes over time due to maturity. In high school it may have been, "What home room do you have?" Later it became, "What do you drive?" In a few years it changes to, "What is your major?" Then it changes again to, "What do you do for a living?" It proceeds to, "What are your thoughts on marriage and children?"

    And for us baby boomers, now it might be, "How many wives (husbands) and grandchildren do you have?" When you're enjoying retirement, it changes again. "How many operations have you had?" And maybe even, "Where do you go for your early bird dinner specials?" Or "What interest rate can you get on a Certificate of Deposit?"

    I am sure we all have acquaintances who have very little maturity. The purpose of this book is to assist BB men to carry themselves in such a manner that they will elevate their ability to get into a "Four C" relationship with a quality BB lady.

    If you are foolish or conceited enough to think that your assets, occupation, amount of hair, or six-pack abs are your credentials for finding a great BB lady, *then you really need this book*. Yes, those are qualifications that might make YOU think you're desirable, but they are not what most BB women value most.

Baby Boomers: Who Are They?

If you do have them, be low key about it. A major turnoff for any BB lady is to ask her, "Wanna go for a ride in my Corvette, Ferrari, Beechcraft, Yacht, or on my Harley?" If that's the best you have to offer, you will inevitably end up with a gold digger or someone even shallower.

If you introduce yourself as Dr. Somebody, or attorney so-and-so, or President of XYZ Company, you are clearly missing the boat.

If you have been blessed with thick hair or have worked out so you still look youthful at the beach, that's great! However, don't admire yourself every time you walk past a mirror!

In other words, get over yourself!

<><><><><>

So, let's start with a definition. Who, exactly, are the baby boomers? This term is used to describe people born roughly between 1946 and 1964. It's basically the group of children born to the servicemen returning from battle in the European and Pacific theaters of World War II. After so many men being away from their families for several years, once the war was over and the servicemen returned home, a lot of babies were born!

So, boomers, this book is for you! If you are single and ready to meet and form a relationship with a QUALITY BB woman, you'll love this book. If you know a BB single man who can't seem to figure out the dating scene, do him a favor: Buy him a copy of this book!

Even if you are a drunken, doper, gambler, conceited, sleezeball, filthy manboy, this book could really change your life. However, if you recognize yourself in this description and admit to being happy as you are, then look for a BB woman

BABY BOOMER WOMEN

who is like you. If that's you, this book is not for you. Don't even read any further.

However, if you are teachable and willing to make some changes, this book will serve as a great guide to follow in finding a wonderful, long-term classy woman. It's not even about change, it's about being willing to modify, adjust and adapt yourself to be able to mold together with the right lady.

One of the wonderful things about BB women is their nationality looks. When boomers were young, there was less mingling of nationalities and races than there is today. A returning Irish serviceman often married an Irish lady and they produced children with Irish facial features: fair skin, freckles, and red hair.

A returning Italian serviceman usually married an Italian gal and they produced Italian looking children with darker complexion, dark hair color, and sculptured facial features. This is generally true for most nationalities, but obviously not all.

I was an exception to the rule. My dad's parents were Italian (from Fano) and my mom's parents were from the Ukraine (Kiev). I sometimes tell folks that I was raised on Kielbasa Parmesan! I suppose we were half-breeds, at least that's what we were called at the time. We felt closer to the Ukrainian community than the Italian community. That was probably a result of a strong, wonderful mother. Neither of my parents were very fluent in their parent's native language. Their parents wanted them to be American, not Ukrainian or Italian. How times have changed!

Although my mom was Orthodox Russian Catholic, her faith wasn't recognized by the Roman Catholic Church. She was forced to study under the Sister of Mercy nuns daily for

Baby Boomers: Who Are They?

months before she was even allowed to convert into Roman Catholicism and thereby have the privilege of a church wedding. My parents were married in 1938 at St. Patrick Church, (later known as St. Patrick Cathedral) in Norwich, Connecticut.

Even more astounding is that the Italian immigrants were considered to be lowlifes by the Catholic Church. The irony! The Catholic Church is headquartered in Rome, their own homeland! The immigrant Italians were even considered by the Church to not be good enough to attend Mass in the main church sanctuary; they were forced to attend Mass in the church's basement! Go Figure!

Personally, I feel that the women born in 1946 and 1947 are the prettiest of all the BB women. They were the first babies whose fathers were returning as veterans of World War II. Could it be that the Great Spirit was rewarding them for their sacrifice, bravery, and duty to their country? Maybe it was from the buildup of hormones due to the loneliness of missing their wives and sweethearts? Their exceptionally good looks are only an observation on my part, not a dis to anyone else.

Many BB children grew up eating foods that were popular from their homeland. Think back, there weren't many Oriental, Mexican, or Middle Eastern restaurants in the 40s and 50s. Today we not only enjoy eating at the fine dining restaurants serving various ethnic foods, but we also have fast food options for Chinese, Sushi, Taco, or Gyro for our convenience. Ethnic food is available on almost every street corner in any major city as well as many small towns. Isn't it wonderful that we now get to taste the best foods from many different cultures?

BABY BOOMER WOMEN

Every generation has been a generation of "firsts." Our grandparents saw the first human flight, first expansion of electricity to the hinterlands, the first mass production of automobiles, and many more.

Our parents saw the first migration of families from the cities to the "burbs," "Rosie the Riveters" working outside of the home, TVs in every living room, and two-car families, to name just a few of their "firsts."

The baby boomer generation has not only a much longer list of firsts, but also our firsts are much more dramatic. These affected society in a much deeper and longer lasting way. Some of our firsts are:

- Women working at jobs traditionally held by men
- Women being college educated in occupations other than teaching and nursing
- Hearing the sound barrier broken
- Seeing a man in space
- Sending men to the moon
- Using a computer
- Having their own cars as teenagers
- Protesting a war and forcing the government to halt it. Remember Country Joe and the Fish? "Be the first one on your block to have your son come home in a box?"
- Enjoying provocative popular music. Remember when Ed Sullivan forced the Rolling Stones to change their lyrics from, "Let's spend the night together" to "Let's spend some time together" on national TV. How about "Up against the wall?"
- Enjoying the national highway system

Baby Boomers: Who Are They?

- Having more than three TV stations and more than one TV in a home
- Enjoying women's Title IX in collegiate sports and then women in professional sports
- Burning their bras and asserting woman's liberation
- Experimenting openly with recreational drugs
- Enjoying concerts like Woodstock (although many were too stoned to remember it)
- Having more than one working career
- Trying different lifestyles, communes, healthful, unfashionable shoes, etc. Do you remember the *I Love Lucy* episode when Ricky blew a fuse because Lucy was taking this new weirdo stuff called ginseng?

These are just a few. There are many more. If you have a moment, listen to the Beatles sing "When I'm Sixty Four." Seems like yesterday when we thought a 64-year-old was a fossil!

Keep in mind that in your search for the right lady they have gone through huge shifts in lifestyles, opinions, and goals. In the 50s they lived under the innocence of America at the time. For many of them, life was like the famous TV shows. Everyone knew *Father Knows Best* or *Leave it to Beaver*. Most baby boomers were raised by parents who were still married to each other. Dad worked and Mom always wore a dress. Mom took care of the household duties; she did not work outside the home.

People had manners, faith, and respect for the government. They dressed more dignified than in more recent years. Sex and innuendo on TV didn't exist. Mary Tyler Moore was the first housewife to wear capris. Lucy and Desi slept in

BABY BOOMER WOMEN

different beds. In the 1950s, uniforms were worn at St. Patrick's School.

Kids went home to change into their play clothes after school before going out for ball games or playtime. Countless studies have proven that student uniforms produce better educated students. Compare that to the clothing kids wear to school today. In the early 60s at the Norwich Free Academy in Norwich, Connecticut, girls were not allowed to wear pants to school unless it was a snowy day. Wearing tee shirts, sweatshirts, and hoodies were absolutely taboo.

I will never forget an experience I had when I was a guest business lecturer in a university. Not even one freshman in the class knew what a subject and predicate were. Yikes! What exactly is being taught today? Yes, they may be proficient at social media, but they can't construct a sentence.

Do you remember when TV stations carried public messages urging people to not leave their keys in their cars because someone might be tempted to steal it? Our family had a beachside summer home about thirty miles from our winter home. Our winter home was left vacant and unlocked for the entire summer for many years. That was just the way everyone lived back then. And yet, there was never anything missing nor was there any other kind of issue. Now that I think about it, we also left our summer home unlocked for the other nine months and there was never an issue with that either. Actually, I'm not even sure there were keys to either house!

Starting around the mid 60s most of that changed. It partially coincided with the influence of the British rock music invasion. The Beatles and Rolling Stones made it chick to have unkempt

Baby Boomers: Who Are They?

long hair, wear nontraditional clothes, be openly rebellious, and use recreational drugs.

Crime began an upswing. The longstanding concept of working for a living began to give way as the government began to teach people they were entitled to the basic necessities without having to work. We began to wonder if rising crime rates might be related to this new entitlement concept.

In the 70s the BB women entered the workforce en masse. Business attire was required; corporate dress codes were enforced. And then along came casual Fridays. Gradually, casual Fridays deteriorated into such casual clothing that you might not be able to differentiate a business person from a street panhandler.

It is essential to understand the life changes that BBs have gone through. Grasping this is a great start in finding that wonderful BB lady! Be flexible enough to live beyond the 1950s but at the same time, don't be so tied to your smart phone that you no longer know how to hold a conversation or handwrite a paragraph!

2
Assess Yourself...
Who Is the Real You?

This is the most difficult part of the book because it requires true introspection and an honest assessment of who you really are. What are your strengths, your beliefs, your thoughts? What are your weaknesses and liabilities?

> You are who you are.

There is an honored naval philosopher who said, "I am what I am and that's all what I am." You may have heard of him – Popeye, the Sailor Man.

Incidentally, Popeye is banned from television because he took a substance that gave him superhuman strength – spinach. Some overeducated, but not practical, psychologist felt that using spinach as a strengthener in the cartoons could lead children to drug addiction. *C'mon folks, let's get real!*

Many people have gone through life lying about themselves for so long they have lost touch with what's true. They actually start to believe their own lies. If this is you, don't feel too bad; most of us have done this to some extent. But if you want a good chance at developing a truly wonderful relationship with a classy BB woman, now's the time to stop telling yourself lies. Throw away all the garbage! Be real!

There are things that you can't or don't want to change. Don't worry about that. The good news is there are many

Assess Yourself... Who Is the Real You?

things that you can modify or at least adjust. Yes, some things are set in concrete, but others can be altered.

Where do you start? With an open mind!

Remember the old saying *when one door closes, another one opens?* The Rev. Dr. Joe Hooper of The Center for Spiritual Living in Palm Desert, California gave me a new spin on it. He said, "When one door closes, lock it up and nail it shut!" Are you still working to open up closed doors? If so, it's time to move on.

There are historical also revisionists. Did FDR actually allow Pearl Harbor to happen? How did the Warren Commission arrive at their ludicrous conclusion about the magic bullet? Is Purgatory ever mentioned anywhere in any scripture?

Do not be a historical revisionist of your own life. It is what it is. Although you may not be proud of everything you're said and done in the past, you must be truthful and proud of who you are today.

Some BB men exaggerate their past lives to ridiculous degrees. Bob said he was a sniper and a helicopter pilot in Vietnam. Does anyone in their right mind believe the United States Army would spend hundreds of thousands of dollars to train a helicopter pilot and then stick him in a hole with a rifle and a long range scope? Yeah, I didn't think so either.

Speaking of Vietnam, I served with Attack Squadron 113 aboard an aircraft carrier, the USS Ranger (CVA 61), on Yankee Station in the Gulf of Tonkin during 1970 and 1971. That experience is deeply burned into my mind. Strangely, sometimes it seems like yesterday and other times it seems like so long ago that it could be someone else's life. Sometimes it even seems like a scene from a movie.

For those of you who are not aware of this, the correct greeting to a Vietnam Vet is not *thank you for your service*. That is nice and does show appreciation for their sacrifices, but the correct way to address any Vietnam Vet is to simply say *welcome home*.

There are a lot of guys who proclaim to be war vets when their actual service was sitting at a desk at Fort Dix. Yes, it's a team effort and the guys manning the desks back home were important to the overall cause; still, let's not confuse the desk jockey with someone who served on the front line. The next time a guy speaks about Vietnam, tell him sincerely that he is *welcome home*!

None of us got the homecoming we rightfully deserved. I have sometimes wondered whatever happened to the hippie chick who spit at me on Broadway in San Diego in 1971. It wouldn't surprise me if she is now serving in Washington and on the taxpayer's payroll. *Just wondering.*

And then, after welcoming him home, ask him what outfit he was in and where he served. These are details that no combat vet will ever forget. If he hesitates even slightly, he is probably full of *feces del toro*!

Jim was a clerk in a city's garbage department. He was a general run-of-the-mill public servant. Today, when Jim speaks and writes about his time working for the city, he claims he was hired to be a department head but was continuously passed over for promotion because he was a whistle blower. He went so far as to write a book about it.

His book? It sold exactly one copy. The city he worked for bought it as evidence in case they decided to sue him.

I worked briefly with Joe, a guy who claimed to have played for the Detroit Tigers. Not in the farm system mind you, but actually in the big leagues. Joe was short, fat, and nowhere near an athlete. Turns out he didn't even know who Al Kaline, Denny McLain, or even Mark Fidrych was. He claimed to be a catcher, yet didn't even know the basics of sending pitch signals to the pitcher. I played catcher at the University of Connecticut, Avery Point in the early 70s and there are some things that still stick in my mind. Things like pitching signals. Some of the basics you just never forget.

So I decided to have a little fun. After listening to Joe's *feces del toro* stories for some time I bet him a thousand dollars; to win the bet, all he had to do was produce his rookie baseball card. That shut him up quickly.

The point is don't exaggerate your past accomplishments.

My dad was an incredible businessman and he often said, "Don't look back on the deals you could have done; be happy with the successful deals you did." There are a lot of could-haves, should-haves, and would-haves in all our lives. Just be truthful because no relationship can flourish when it's based on lies.

Do some ruthless honest self-assessment.

What are your strengths? What are your weaknesses? You'd better be truthful with yourself here because these are topics that will eventually be discussed with a lady on some future date. What characteristics do you possess that make you proud? Which ones need some work? Are you willing to work on them? At our age, people don't change a lot but there is some amount of modification and adaptation necessary for any relationship to develop.

The #1 deal-breaker

The biggest obstacle in starting a meaningful relationship is the state of their spiritual life. Although some may still deny this, all of us have some form of spirituality. Sometimes, but not always, spirituality is displayed in churches or other houses of worship. Sometimes it is completely internal.

Some religions forbid marrying outside of the religion and there are others who are more liberal in that. However, most agree that marrying within their common religion gives the marriage a better chance of long-term success.

Start with the wedding itself. Is it at the Cathedral, Temple, or on a cruise ship? What religion will the ceremony be associated with? Who will officiate the ceremony? This is just the tip of the iceberg, even before you say "I do."

There is a very funny French comedy series called "Kabul Kitchen." There is an episode where a Frenchman is forced to convert to Islam against his will, in order to marry the powerful drug lord's daughter. Hilarious!

Back to the seriousness of this subject. If there is a significant disparity is the spiritual lives and levels of the people involved, they should definitely be addressed in the early stages of a relationship. There could be future issues such as, which religion will the children be taught? What religious holidays will be celebrated in the home? What is your degree of depth in your own church's teachings? Are you fervent about it or more casual?

This is not to say that mixed religion marriages don't work; there are many examples that show they can and do work.

But, individuals who are on the extreme ends of their respective religions should look within that particular community for a potential mate. Be honest with yourself and each other on this one. It's #1.

The #2 deal-breaker

Okay, so you may have some huge weaknesses. For example, if you are a tobacco addict, you will not attract any BB woman unless she shares a nicotine addiction also. Actually, it is rather difficult to find one because most nicotine addicts are already dead or well on the path of self-induced death. Tobacco use is not a fashionable fad, nor a way to control stress. Are you so uninformed to simply call it a bad habit?

Many clinical studies have proven that nicotine is the strongest addictive substance on earth; far stronger than alcohol, cocaine, or even heroin. A big thanks goes out to the elected traitors serving in Washington who got elected with the help of huge donations from the tobacco companies. Ever wonder how many deaths were caused by those lying tobacco executives who slipped millions to the dirty traitor politicians? *Millions!* My own mother was a victim of their deception. Remember when LSMFT meant Lucky Strike Means Fine Tobacco!

There were experiments done with lab animals and nicotine. The researchers would put food and nicotine in the animal's cage and later remove it. Once the animal tried the nicotine, they quickly became addicted to it. Although the food was right there, guess what they died from?

STARVATION! They actually died from starvation.

The food was right there but over and over, they chose the nicotine and certain death instead of food and life.

I have personally seen people smoking while hooked up to chemo bags. I have heard that some smokers actually smoked through their tracheotomy holes in their lungs! Let's thank those lying tobacco company presidents who swore to congress under oath that tobacco wasn't harmful. Congratulations also to the traitors in Congress who agreed! Check your retirement plans and mutual funds. Do you unknowingly own tobacco company stocks? Shame on you if you do.

Every BB woman I ever met said tobacco use is a major deal-breaker.

The #3 deal-breaker?

Are you curious about the #3 deal-breaker? Maybe you'll guess this one. Over-indulgence of alcohol.

A glass or two of wine, even daily, is fine. That's something most BB women enjoy. However, hammering down shots of Tequila or beer bonging is definitely the #3 deal-breaker for BB women. This is part of that tell-yourself-the-truth we talked about. You're going to want to be honest here.

For many women, even a convenience store beer in the car is unacceptable. To risk a DUI is foolhardy. The legal costs to fight a DUI can easily run into the thousands and, of course, there are further ramifications. I am an FAA licensed private pilot and I would lose that license if I were ever convicted of a single DUI. In some cases, a DUI conviction could result in being fired from your job. Incidentally, the Canadians deserve kudos in this regard. I have never met a Canadian who will drink and drive.

Mike met a very pretty, shapely, happy BB lady. She enjoyed a couple glasses of wine daily and sometimes more. Somehow, Mike didn't notice the pattern. She had cleverly hidden the clues from him. She would hide her small nip bottles of wine in the toilet tank, the washed out detergent

Assess Yourself... Who Is the Real You?

containers, the trees in the yard, and even tucked into some of his seldom worn clothes. The fact that she was doing so much hiding meant she absolutely knew she had a problem. Her drinking actually started in the morning but the white wine left no telltale signs.

Eventually they married. Mike, thinking he was Mr. Macho Man, felt that his love for her would be enough to overcome all and that he could help her to control the alcohol.

WRONG!

Her drinking was the #1 priority in her life. Mike was never going to be her priority. His great love for her wasn't enough. The end results were not pretty. His world became filled with disasters.

There were failed attempts at rehab, loss of her driver's license (although even after that she continued to drive illegally), loss of jobs, a hit-and-run on a police officer (yeah, read that again if you need to), and several arrests. There was time spent in jail.

Eventually, Mike was able to obtain a LIFETIME restraining order against her and he began the slow, painful process of working his way through a very painful divorce.

In many states the allowable blood alcohol level limit is .08%. When she died, her blood alcohol level was .46%, nearly *six times* the legal limit. She drank herself to an early death.

Because alcoholics can be very devious about hiding possible clues, you really need to keep your eyes open for possible signs. Think about it. When an alcoholic is sober, she can be vivacious, full of laughter, and ready to dance, play, and ride her motorcycle. Who isn't drawn to such a woman? Mike's wife was all that. She especially loved her three children, but even the thought of never seeing her grandchildren again wasn't enough for her to conquer her alcoholism. Although it was truly a shame that she died too early, it may have been a blessing. Clearly she could have killed someone on the roads.

It is encouraging to see the number of states (including our nation's capital, Washington, DC) that have relaxed or changed cannabis laws. It's even more encouraging to see the medical breakthroughs concerning non-euphoric cannabis oil (CBD).

And deal-breaker #4 is:
After alcohol; the next deal breaker is drug use. This could be an obvious or a subtle problem. At the Boomer age bracket, most of the hard drug users are already dead. However, there is another more widespread epidemic – prescription drug abuse. This addiction can be hard to detect since it's basically legal if you know an unscrupulous physician who will write unneeded scripts.

Carla was a tall, slender, attractive lady with tons of energy. Her secret to maintaining her slender physique was unknown even to her family. She was hooked on amphetamines or tranquilizers, which she got by swapping sex for prescriptions. Her only friends were doctor's wives because they could get their husbands to write unnecessary prescriptions.

I know health care professionals may find this disturbing, but it happens every day all over America.

One more deal-breaker
There is another potential deal-breaker you need to be aware of. This is one that has become more commonplace with the advent of casinos. You guessed it: a gambling addiction. In

Assess Yourself... Who Is the Real You?

the past, gambling addicts would lose their money to the bookies, back alley sports betting, or at high stakes card games.

Today the action is 24 hours a day, 365 days a year. There are private casinos and there are tribal casinos on Native American tribal lands. These are considered to be foreign entities, and therefore not under the jurisdiction of U.S. laws. In reality, many of the tribal casinos are actually financed by outside investors with profits split between the investors and the tribal nations.

You may be skeptical about this but studies have shown there is a higher percentage of women gambling addicts than men. Additionally, there is a high rate of addicted gamblers in the senior citizen segment of the general population. There are stories of senior citizens who actually soil themselves while sitting for mindless hours playing slot machines. Why? Because they are so blinded by their addiction, they actually, foolishly "just know" that the jackpot is coming on the next pull. They aren't able to get up and walk away.

Interestingly, slots are the backbone of the gaming industry. Slots bring in more money than all the other gambling games. Remember this: the less you have to think about the type of gambling you are doing, the lower the odds are of winning. What could be easier than simply putting your money in and pulling a handle? It's mindlessly monotonous and repetitive.

Most professional gamblers will say the best odds of winning are at the roulette table. If you play the colors, your chances of winning are almost 50-50.

I was at a huge casino with a date one day because we received a complimentary suite from one of the Native American contractors. I learned a lot about my date that night. We spotted a section of penny slot machines. We deposited the minimum ($5) and she started to pull the handle. In less than two minutes she stopped and turned to look at me. "What do we have to do to lose our $5 and get out of this noisy, ridiculous place?" We bet it all on the next pull, lost it all, and then went happily around the casino enjoying the food and the night life.

Do I have to tell you, this woman scored points with me that night!

My Native American contractor buddy offered to take us up to the "High Rollers Lounge" where all the food and drinks are complimentary. Right next to the elevator, there was a big bruiser guy, a well dressed security guard. He had one job: to ensure that only the high rollers got on the elevator! Okay, so – a $20 tip!

Then we rode up the exclusive elevator with no stops all the way to top floor, which is where the High Rollers Lounge was. Upon exiting the elevator, there was another huge bruiser to greet us – another $20 tip. I was introduced then to the bartender – another $20 tip! After that, I was introduced to the carving chef. Can you guess? Another $20 tip! Lastly, I was introduced to the cocktail waitress, and yep – another $20 tip!

It cost me $100 to eat for free that night!

I still laugh every time I think about that date.

Now consider your potential mate.

What are the characteristics, strengths, and weaknesses you are looking for in a mate? There are countless jokes about finding a woman who is rich, beautiful, well shaped, and incredibly erotic.

They are just jokes.

Assess Yourself... Who Is the Real You?

Paul was a friend of mine who, quite by chance, met a BB lady at a dance. This was a lady who really had it all going for her. She was beyond beautiful, shapely, financially successful, and a terrific intimacy partner. Although at first it didn't look likely that they would become a couple, slowly, things did start to gel.

Over time, she taught him how to filter himself (more on that later), and they got along very well. She did not live in the state where they met, but because things were going so well, they continued on a 2,200 mile, long distance relationship.

Eventually, they moved in together. She was an astute business person and actually started a new business that he could operate, allowing him to be financially successful. He became the daily bread winner.

This wonderful relationship lasted two years. The business connection lasted two more years until it became apparent there were other irresolvable issues. They had different long-term goals that were magnified one day when Paul had an outburst that should never have happened. Eventually, the business was sold and they parted ways.

The lesson to be learned here is that even if some potential partner may appear to be everything you could want in a partner, it may not always work. Paul and his girlfriend have since moved on but are on friendly terms to this day. Everyone is in your life for a reason.

Tony met a BB lady through the internet. She was a widow and in addition to the fact that she personally had a successful professional career, her deceased husband left her rather well off. She was somewhat shy and had a rather nice, but dated appearance. He gently convinced her to change her hair to a more modern style. He even helped her to update her wardrobe, which had become matronly. Her intimacy experiences were limited and he brought her to new levels in that regard too. She was extremely generous but was constantly concerned about her wealth. It turned out this became the reason they broke up. Money should not be a consideration in a relationship unless there is a huge gap in each other's assets. Everybody is in your life for a reason.

The point is, don't let money influence you too much in either direction.

Vincent met a great BB lady at her place of employment. She was tall, knock-out beautiful, and had an incredible shape. She had been a model in her early days and even in her late 60s she was still doing some modeling. Although they shared a great admiration for each other physically, they did not share the same core values. Having the same core values is essential to a great relationship. They struggled financially until they both lost respect for each other and eventually parted ways.

Here's the point: exterior looks are less meaningful than then other deeper characteristics that are needed in a happy relationship.

Let's review.

Are your strengths and weaknesses such that each partner can support the other emotionally when needed? Are your fears and expectations compatible with hers? Compatibility goes a long way, but sometimes "two peas in a pod" doesn't work. When one is down, the other has to help pick the partner up.

Don't look for the perfect person. Discover the one with whom you are the most *compatible*.

Compliment your lady often, but always sincerely. Compliments about outward appearances are important, but nowhere near as important as complimenting her on her

Assess Yourself... Who Is the Real You?

inward beauty. *You're wonderful at just being you! Thank you* or *I appreciate what you just did or said* are words that should be repeated often.

By now, you should have a good start at completing an honest assessment of yourself. You should also be developing a good idea of the qualities you are looking for in a lady. You may even have some conversation starters to get the ball rolling.

All of these are great but there are four attributes which are absolute requirements for finding happiness with any BB woman. Remember these?

Grooming/Hygiene

Manners

Loyalty

Integrity

3
Before Meeting Them

Ready to meet someone? Good! Now let's review some basic hygiene. Yes, this is really basic, but what could be more important?

General body hygiene

An attractive appearance does not necessarily mean you must always be spit shined from head to toe. After mowing the lawn or doing some "honey do" projects, you'll look different than when you are on a date or meeting socially with friends.

The following are requirements if you want to maintain a lasting relationship with a BB woman. Some are not absolutely critical but the first few cannot ever be ignored. EVER!

If you have been single for any period of time, you may have gotten lazy about some basic hygiene habits. We're guys. It happens.

Well, okay. But now's the time to get back on track. Immediately!

Daily showering is a must. In addition, showering after any sweaty activity, after being in the pool, or after any physical exertion, is a must. Even if you think it is only slightly needed, a shower before a date is also required. This is not the time to cut corners. Use a wash cloth or a skin scrubber to cleanse yourself. Don't just use your hands; they won't remove the dead skin cells effectively. Scrub!

Use a soap of your choice but nothing with too much scent. Many men prefer using liquid body wash instead of bar soap claiming that the reuse of bar soap allows germs to remain on the soap and eventually back on their bodies. If you do use bar soap, rinse it off after every use.

The same rule applies to your deodorant or antiperspirant. A natural type is better because most commercial products contain aluminum, which has been linked to Alzheimer's disease. (It makes me wonder about the long-term effects of drinking perked coffee from those old-fashioned aluminum coffee pots. It's what our parents drank every day.)

Be cautious in the use of aftershave and especially cologne. Most aftershave products contain a high percentage of alcohol, which only close the skin's pores after shaving. There are stories of some extreme alcohol addicts who have actually drunk cologne in an attempt to soothe their addictive cravings. Wow!

You may want to consider using a balm of some sort that contains lotions or oils to aid in keeping the skin supple and healthy. Again, try to find natural products as opposed to the ones made in a lab from chemicals.

Have you ever stood in a supermarket behind an older person with an unmistakable disgusting urine smell? Or someone who overdosed themselves with perfume or cologne?

Yuk. Double yuk!

Do not allow yourself to be that person. You may be surprised to learn that many BB women do not especially like cologne and are attracted to a man's natural pheromone scent. Eventually, you'll learn the preference of your lady.

And then? Whatever aroma your lady likes, that's what you wear. Wear cologne that she likes or none at all if that's her desire. She may suggest some or even offer to give you some as a gift. In any event, your personal aroma should be her choice, not yours.

BABY BOOMER WOMEN

There are probably some so-called "tough guys" reading this who have never given a thought to the following but here is another bit of advice that might be new for BB men.

Get a facial.

Facials are not only for ladies but also for men. You don't have to get it done often but it has great results. Facials are available at most day spas and the cost is minimal considering the improvement in your facial skin appearance. A good skin technician will use hot cloths or steam to open your pores, thoroughly scrub your skin for cleanliness, and then she will remove all the dead skin, blackheads, and pimples, etc.

Next, she'll use various oils or lotions to revive your skin. Make sure you give yourself a very close shave before getting a facial and discuss exactly what the tech will be doing before proceeding. If you have never had a facial, I think you will be surprised and pleased with the outcome.

Another way to keep that look of vitality is to get massages. It's not about just getting one from some relative or a recent graduate from massage school, but from one who is highly trained and effective in their treatment. Effective massages relieve stress as well as improve your posture, etc. Having good posture and an upright walk exemplify good health and youthfulness.

I have mentioned natural products a few times and you will pick up more of this concept in upcoming chapters. I am sure you are aware that when commercial food producers want to fool us, their slick marketing people come up with a catchy description. One of their favorite tricks is to use the word "lite." Lite this and lite that. What a bunch of *feces del toro* that is!

The word "lite" has no actual meaning. There are no guidelines or legal requirements in using the word "lite" to describe a product. Fortunately, this scam has been exposed and most consumers are rarely fooled by it today.

Beer makers produce "lite" beer. Ever wonder how they do that? What's the secret?

They simply add more water! Wow. Imagine that!

There was a cookie maker who made cookies out of two wafers with a sugary filling in the middle. They tried to hoodwink the public by producing a "lite" version of their cookies by simply reducing the amount of the sugary filling by a minute percentage. What a scam!

Now this same scheme has hit the word "natural." For something to be classified as natural, the government says it only has to have 85% natural ingredients. The remaining 15% can be any kind of schmutz the processor wants to add in, while still keeping the label "natural."

For this outrageous scam, give thanks to the lobbyists who are paid by the companies to control our elected officials in Washington. We elect them to represent us and instead they spend a quarter of their time raising money for their respective parties instead of representing their constituents. To me, that is a classic textbook definition of the word traitor. Where else can you work for two years and get full pay and full benefits for a lifetime? Can you imagine running any business like that? No wonder America is approaching bankruptcy. Just have the Fed print more bongo bucks and if you have your head in the sand, it'll all just go away!

Well, off the soapbox and back to grooming.

Oral hygiene

There are many other factors in considering hygiene in addition to basic showering. Oral hygiene is absolutely critical. Nobody – absolutely nobody gets to be with a BB woman if he has bad breath. This cannot be overstressed. You and I know this, of course, so now let's talk about what to do!

The prevention and remedies for bad breath includes not only thorough brushing but also flossing and water picking regularly. You should also scrape film from your tongue. There is no substitute for regular dental care. Remember the old saying: Be true to your teeth and they won't be false to you!

If you have chronic bad breath it could be from some oral or stomach disorder. Definitely have that checked by your dentist or physician.

Don't miss breath care, especially after a spicy garlic dinner. This calls for extra help. Use something to ensure your breath is fresh and appealing. There are many types of discrete breath sprays and mints that are effective. Always keep a container of mints in your pocket or in your car's console. You always want to have fresh breath so you are ready for any opportunity to get close to a BB lady.

Your teeth

Your teeth are the centerpiece of your smile and your smile is your personal introduction card. If you have visual cavities, missing teeth, badly misaligned teeth, or yellowing teeth, correct those situations immediately. There are all kinds of dental insurance plans that allow payment plans. There is no excuse for you. Keep your teeth and gums healthy.

It is becoming more common for adults to have orthodontic work. Payment plans are available, and options are numerous. Some types of braces hardly even show. If your teeth are in really bad shape, consider caps or implants; both are available through new dental technology. Of course, the down side is that some of those remedies can be pretty pricey.

However, there is an alternative. I had to have two crowns replaced. The price in Florida was $3188. I got the same dental work done with excellent results in Mexico for just $600! If you go this route, just make sure you have recommendations from other patients at the dentist you choose.

Everyone's teeth gradually become yellow with time. The good news is more options than ever are now available to you. Simple yellowing can be improved by at-home, do-it-yourself whitening kits or you can have it done professionally by your dental hygienist. There are also teeth whitening technicians who specialize in whitening solutions done on a one-time treatment basis. They are very effective and they last quite a while, depending on the amount of coffee, red wine, or tobacco you use.

At one point in my property management career, I managed a commercial complex located on a hospital campus. I had an employee there who was an excellent worker and a great guy. However, his entire mouth was filled with visible rotting, yellowed teeth. It was hard to look at him. For whatever reason, he refused to go to a dentist. The irony of it was that he refused to eat at the hospital cafeteria because he felt that the food had bad germs in it. He also refused to acknowledge that his oral diseases were contributing to the decline in his general health.

What a walking contradiction! His mouth germs were ruining his general health but he refused to eat in the hospital cafeteria because the food wasn't clean enough for him! Go figure! Because of his severe dental appearance, I eventually transferred him to a position where he did not interact with people who could actually see his bad teeth.

I knew of a lady once who was very impressed that a man kept dental floss in his car's console. She didn't want him to use it in her presence but it was nice to know it was there in case of an emergency when something got stuck in someone's teeth.

Now, about your hair

Your hair completes your facial appearance. Very few of us have the same head of hair we had in our earlier years. I tell my barber I want the tweezer cut. Just pluck off a few of the ones on the top that are still remaining!

Actually, my barber has an express chair, just like in the supermarket. For twelve hairs or less!

Those BB men who still have a full head of hair at our age are indeed lucky. I am still waiting for medical breakthroughs that will allow whole hairy scalps to be transplanted. Then all I will have to do is find somebody who will leave me his hair in his will! I know, pretty farfetched and unnecessary!

If you are concerned about thinning or loss of hair, the first and foremost guideline is, if you wear your hair as a comb-over, you forfeit your man card immediately! You have fooled no one but yourself.

Many BB women say that comb-over hair on men reminds them of Snoopy (from Peanuts comics) sitting on top of his doghouse pretending to be a pilot flying with his scarf flowing in the wind behind him! Maybe a comb-over guy should ride in a convertible with the top down to realize how ridiculous this style is. Believe me on this: a comb-over is for an insecure,

Before Meeting Them

uninformed guy. If you are open to having BB women laugh at you, then go for it.

The next consideration is hair plugs. I understand that they are expensive and painful during the transplant process. There is improving technology in this area and when completed, it may be a very effective solution. The downside is that you sometimes look like you have corn rows while going through the treatments.

One of the most common ways men try to hide their baldness is with a toupee (commonly referred to as a "rug"). There are very few rugs that actually look like hair. Granted, there are a few, but they are very, very few. The rug salesman will tell you to wear a hat for quite a while before you unveil your rug and presumably after that, people will forget you were once bald. Presto! They will think the rug is actually your own real hair. If they can make you believe that, they might also have the Brooklyn Bridge for sale.

In the event you do have a rug and you meet a BB lady you'd like to develop a relationship with, I suggest being honest from the start. Tell her the truth. If you don't tell her beforehand and someday she gets to the point where she touches your rug, she will know what it is immediately. If you already told her, she will appreciate that you are truthful and sincere and not trying to fool her in any way. BB women are experienced in many ways and are worldly smart. At the end of the day, honesty will always be appreciated.

Being truthful with yourself is always a good thing too. If the relationship starts to develop, ask her if she would like to see you without it. She may surprise you and like you for just being yourself.

I have hair on the sides of my head but have only a few surviving hairs on top. I call it the Elmer Fudd hairdo! Sometimes when I meet a new woman, I go straight for humor. "Is my toupee on straight?" It usually gets a laugh. It's an honest appraisal of myself and a good ice-breaker.

In the past, many Hollywood stars were required to wear rugs because the movie viewing public lived in such a fantasy world. That fantasy meant that for men to be handsome and sexy, they had to have hair. If you look closely at some older movies, it is apparent that the toupee business in Hollywood was very lucrative. The list is long but look closely at Joe Cool, The Duke, Serpico, 007, Columbo, Ole' Blue Eyes, just to name a few. Hollywood producers would like to have you believe that baldness never happens in Tinseltown.

Greg had a wife who eventually lost all her hair due to chemotherapy. What did Greg do? He had his head shaved in a show of empathy for his wife. As part of his job, he gave presentations and speeches concerning his profession.

At one presentation in a swanky hotel, Greg was the keynote speaker, seated at the head table with other dignitaries. On his right was a couple he had known professionally for several years. She was a BB model type: tall, lanky, very pretty, and always tastefully dressed. Her husband was a retired Navy Commander who had commanded a destroyer and a tour in the Gulf of Tonkin. He was quite a guy and a true military warrior. She sat to the right of Greg and her husband sat on her right side at the head table. As they chatted, she asked about Greg's wife. She thought he looked handsome with his head clean shaven. She went on to say that her husband also had thinning hair and she wished he would shave it off completely, but he refused to do so. Greg asked her why she (and many other women) found baldness to be attractive. She said it was the confidence bald men so often have. It was the this-is-what-I-am, take-it-or-leave-it attitude she found to be appealing.

As the conversation progressed, she asked if she could rub his head. It seemed a little odd to him at the time, especially with two hundred people in attendance, but he agreed. She rubbed it playfully for a short moment until Greg began to sense she was enjoying it a little too much. By then he wanted to get out of a weird situation, so he excused himself to head to the restroom.

So, remember this: Some women do like bald men. Ask Yul Brenner or Howie Mandel.

OK, let's say you do have a good head of hair. First, let's address some potential problems.

Are you wearing a style that looks like you are trying to recapture your youth? Do you still have rock star ridiculous long hair? How about a mullet or a ponytail? If so, find a lady who is attracted to that appearance. I have always found it amusing that some BB guys with thinning white hair wear that thin hair in a ponytail. I mean, really? Twenty hairs on top and white hair down to his shoulders? Yikes!

Find a BB lady who is straightforward enough to tell you the truth. You might like that ponytail, but most BB women probably won't. So, make a decision. Keep that decades old hair style? Or update your hair style to something that won't chase away women? It's your choice. An improved appearance will increase your chancing of finding a quality BB lady.

Of course, all of us would probably like to look a little younger than we actually are. This is especially true with hair color. There are some BB men who look terrific with the Silver Fox look, but they are in the minority. This is also true for BB women. A few BB women who have healthy thick hair may look good in silver, but not white hair color. However, most BBs look either old or matronly with white hair.

This is one of the easiest things to remedy. Simple and easy. Although you won't find hair coloring offered in barber shops (it's prohibited), nearly every hair salon does it every day. You can also do it yourself at home. Many salons have coloring that allows for a subtle blend of gray along with your own natural color. Many at-home products allow for color blending as well.

At our age, to have all jet black hair is second only to a comb-over on the ridiculous scale. Remember, you are trying a find a quality BB lady, so act and look accordingly.

Facial hair

I kept a moustache for thirty-three years. It was full and mostly bushy and it made me look like the Italian version of Stalin! At this point in life I think most BB women prefer their BB men to be clean shaven. Of course, there always exceptions.

Here's something I don't get: What is it with the youthful unshaven look popularized decades ago on the Miami Vice show? Don't women care about whisker burns anymore?

It appears that upon retirement many BB men grow facial hair to show what a rebel tough guy they are, when in reality, most of them were robots controlled by their respective corporate cultures.

Road machines

What's even more hilarious is when guys buy themselves some fat road-noisy motorcycle to further emphasize what tough guys they think have now become. During Daytona Beach Bike Week, they are laughingly referred to as Rolex Riders because

Before Meeting Them

very few of them can properly ride their new two-wheeled toys. They are afraid to lean over, they miss shifting of gears, and they don't have the ability to ride slowly in congested city traffic.

I have had seventeen motorcycles in my lifetime, starting when I was nineteen years old. Although I do enjoy motorcycles, I am not, nor have I ever considered myself to be a biker. About two-thirds of my bikes have been off-road machines because I used to participate in Enduro off-road racing. I wonder how many old geezer macho biker types could race fifty to a hundred miles through the woods. It is definitely a young man's sport.

Even more outrageous is European Ice Racing. One of my former employees, Mike Burnham of Lebanon, Connecticut, is one of only a handful of Americans who have ever even trained for it, let alone participate in it. They race on the same ice tracks as speed skaters, four racers to a heat. It is ladder competition with the winner of each heat continuing on until someone is named the winner.

The bikes are 500cc, two-stroke. They burn alcohol as fuel. The spikes are on the right half of each tire and extend out about an inch-and-a-half. Because European Ice Racing has riders leaning down so far in the corners, there is no peg on the left side. The left handlebar is rounded off at the tip so it won't dig into the ice when the rider leans so far down, the handlebar touches the ice. There are two speeds: start and go, and there are no brakes! True madness!

I used to think a motorcycle demolition derby was insane, but nothing compares to European Ice Racing! I would love to see any macho road biker even attempt this! They probably couldn't even make it through the first turn!

Sorry... I got sidetracked with old geezers with beards riding their noisy, silly road bikes.

Back to grooming...

There are other more subtle areas of grooming that make a difference in appearance. One that is often missed is the fingernails. You need clean, well-clipped fingernails. You will strike out immediately if you have dirt showing under your nails or if your nails need to be trimmed. Please don't even start me on the ugliness of nails being bitten down to the skin. Ugh. Very unattractive!

A manicure is not just for women. Don't be afraid to try it. Also, some BB women like to include toes in bed playtime. If that is the case, definitely get a pedicure.

Now, let's talk about some less common hygiene items. Keep your nose hairs, ear hairs, and eyebrows trimmed. During my time in the military, I once served under a commander who actually had waxed handlebar eyebrows. I often wondered how he got away with that.

How about your shoes? If you're wearing leather shoes, they need to be shined. Granted that sandals, sneakers (remember that's what we wore before they were called athletic shoes), and flip flops are more popular today. However, if you do have any leather shoes or dress shoes, keep them shined. Even if you just use some cheap liquid polish, keep them shined.

In the airport in Columbia, South Carolina, there used to be some shoeshine guys who could actually make a tune out of snapping the buffing rag in a certain way. It was absolutely amazing.

I once knew a BB lady who loved the fact that her guy used shoe trees and kept his shoes shined!

Before Meeting Them

Eric was a guy who always dressed the same. It was like his own personal uniform: skuzzy, stretched out, brown tee shirt, with baggy soiled jeans and dirty sneakers. Eric's friend suggested that he clean up a little, to which he replied, "I like to look like a bum." He dresses like this 98% of the time. Do you know what the BB women call him? "Dirty Eric." Isn't that a nickname to be proud of?

Eric once went to a New Year's Eve event dressed in his usual "uniform." I know this because I was there! I was with a lovely BB lady as my date. It was New Year's Eve, so I wore a tux and my date was beyond stunning in a beautiful formal dress with classy hair, nails, and jewelry to top it all off. She was truly breath-taking. Her appearance was absolutely red-carpet-ready and "Dirty Eric" showed up looking like he just crawled out of the sewer. My date was not snooty but she did say she would never attend that New Year's Eve event again unless a dress code was enforced.

Keep your wardrobe up-to-date. When something is worn out, throw it away or donate it to charity, no matter how attached to it you are. If you are on a budget, find some thrift stores, consignment shops, or even yard sales. They are some of the best-kept secrets to dressing well on a budget. You might have to do a little hunting, but these are good ways to get inexpensive, upscale clothes.

Thrift stores provide a wide assortment of great clothing. If you're looking for quality, find thrift stores located in more affluent areas. Areas of higher priced housing are where people live who have finer, nicer wardrobes. They upgrade their clothing more often. It's definitely a win for you.

BABY BOOMER WOMEN

Another quick word about dressing properly. If you have a large tummy or even worse, a full fledged beer belly, try this. Do NOT wear form fitting shirts! They only accentuate your tummy. As with many of us, it's bigger than it was 30 years ago, so no need to parade around with it hanging out.

There is an easy way to disguise it. Wear looser fitting shirts and let the tails hang out over your belt. This also goes for men with a large waist line who wear their belts low so their stomach hangs over their belt. How gross! Just let your shirt tails camouflage your belly. If you do have a gut, do NOT tuck your shirt into your pants with your belt showing. If you can't see that this is an issue, look at Santa with his big black belt covering his big red jacketed belly.

If you are fortunate and have exercised enough to have a reasonably flat stomach, good for you. You can wear more form fitting clothing. But if you have a big fat gut or a beer belly, start now! Do something about it. The only women who would accept a beer belly appearance in a new date are the ones who are overweight and sloppy themselves.

Morbidly obese people are draining the health care system due to the extra health issues caused by their gluttony. There used to be excuses like, "They have a glandular problem." Yes, I agree, they have a gland in their arm that keeps forcing Twinkies (and other garbage food) down their throats. When I go to the VA for medical treatment, I see it all. It must be an epidemic because there are many, many obese vets there. It upsets me that those who really need health care are sidelined by the obese ones who are often... guess what? Cigarette smokers too! When I encounter a big fat guy at the VA, I usually try to offer a mock compliment. I tell them that it appears they are doing a really good job... with their anorexia. Shockingly, some don't even understand that I am insulting them.

Before Meeting Them

Karen once bought a beautiful wedding gown designed by a famous designer at a thrift shop in a very affluent area. It had only been worn once. Because Karen had surgically enhanced her shape, she took it to a dressmaker to have the dress altered. It is a lot of work to alter a wedding gown. It requires a highly skilled professional. When Karen asked what it would cost, the seamstress said she would do it for free! Shocked, Karen didn't even know what to say.

The dressmaker explained, if Karen would allow her to cut out the designer tag, she could sew the tag into one of her other customer's dresses. Her other client would then have bragging rights because of the designer label. Karen's wedding dress originally cost $6,500, but she bought it for $100! What a great deal!

As one comedian said, "Ever notice that the majority of the great designers are Italian or French? A woman will boastfully say that she is wearing her "Versace gown."

You may ask why there are no Israeli fashion designers. Would she say, "I'm wearing my Goldberg?" Would a female terrorist say she's wearing her fashionable flack vest designed by Abdullah?

Everyone has their own individual look and style, but always remember that usually impeccable grooming and a warm sincere smile will at least get you in the door.

My mom used to say, "The way you dress in public is a good indication of what you think of yourself."

Thanks, mom!

4
Where to Meet Them

How many times have you heard, "I just don't know any good places to meet someone special."

If that's you, it's obvious you're not going to the right places. BB women are everywhere and often there are many more women than men. Statistically, there are more widows than widowers. We're told that 40 is the new 60, meaning that many 60-year-olds look like they are in their 40s.

Well, even that has changed. I know several women in their early 70s who look like they are in their mid-50s! The percentages are on the BB man's side in finding a great BB lady. They are out there, but where do you meet one?

Rule#1: *Don't sit on your lazy butt, watching the mind farts on network TV!*

If you don't already understand that network TV is the trash that it is, slap yourself in the face and wake up! Granted, there are a few shows with redeeming qualities but you really have to search for them. Even if the program's content is acceptable, the commercials insult anyone with a working brain.

Okay, no extra charge for that. Let's continue.

On the other hand, public TV offers a wide range of programming without commercial interruption. Personally, I have a small (5x5 inch) antenna that receives fifty stations, twenty of which actually carry pretty good programming. The one-time charge for antennas ranges from $10 to about $75. It's certainly a much better deal than the inflated cable prices.

Go to TVFOOL.COM, punch in your address and it will give you the signal strength of each station in your area.

Regarding public TV programming, the European police and detective suspense shows are far superior to their American counterparts.

Look up MHz Networks; their programming is terrific! No commercials make for enjoyable entertainment and yes, they are subtitled. However, the twists and turns of their plots are well written and actually believable.

The content of America's crime shows is so bizarre that I have often wondered if the writers are descendents of Hannibal Letcher or Charlie Manson. I once saw part of a show where the killer was adding his victim's amputated fingertips to the lemonade being served to the volunteer search party. Who writes this stuff? Yikes!

Have you ever noticed that the scenes in American TV are so much shorter than they used to be? Sometimes they are so fast that we geezers can hardly follow them.

Boom! Bang! Zip! Next scene...

If you really do like to watch NCAA or professional sports on TV, at least go out of the house to do so. Sports bars are everywhere and there you can root for your teams with fellow fans or you might even meet a lady there.

If you are dating a BB lady and still watch sports, let her enjoy her time away from you. When she returns after the game, ask her to share her time away and be enthusiastic about sharing her enjoyment. Don't make it an interrogation; just let it be sharing life's experiences together.

For example, if she went shopping, ask her if she found anything new. You might even ask her to try it on and compliment her on how wonderful it looks. If she played golf, ask her for her score and were her drives better than her putts? On what hole did she score the best?

Another detriment to being a TV couch potato is that one tends to munch while watching TV. Beer, soda, popcorn, chips with salsa or dip, ice cream, nuts. Yikes, calculate those calories!

The downside of beer is twofold. Many alcoholics hide behind, "Well, it's only beer." Duh, sure! The second is the calorie count. Simply look at the waist line of habitual beer drinkers. It's just not a pretty sight, even worse in the nude. Does anyone think a BB lady is attracted to a big fat beer belly? I doubt it!

Soda is poison. Let's start with sugar. A twelve ounce soda has the equivalent of twelve spoons of sugar. It's as much sugar as four glazed doughnuts!

But it's not only the calories in soda, there is the sodium benzoate and caffeine to consider. Although diet soda does have fewer calories, it usually contains aspartame, a laboratory poison. Your body fools itself and one does not actually lose weight drinking it. There are many clinical studies that prove this. Since it is a poison, it is also addictive. A recent U.S. President was said to drink up to ten diet sodas a day!

Take your doctor's advice and drink water. However, it must be spring water. Filtered water doesn't cut it. The commercial water filter salesmen would have you think that their product will purify anything (even sewer water). This is simply not true.

Most municipal drinking water contains fluoride, which is a by-product of the phosphate industry. It's used as the basis for fertilizer but the fluoride must first be removed because it is a poison. It might actually kill the plants instead of helping them grow. Gee, that sounds healthy, doesn't it?

Where to Meet Them

The U.S. is the only developed country where fluoride is allowed to be added into the drinking water. In recent years there have been petitions signed by scientists at the U.S. Food & Drug Administration. Due to their efforts, along with grass root health groups, the legal fluoride levels have been lowered. I hope someday fluoride will be eliminated from our water entirely.

Fluoride may be acceptable in toothpaste for preventing tooth decay, but ingesting fluoride has been linked to bad health and premature death. Just drink the water Mother Earth has provided for us.

One more note about fluoride. Way back in the 1950s, one doctor in my hometown of Norwich, Connecticut was brave enough to speak out against fluoride. Although this man was a health genius and intellectually years ahead of others in his field, he was openly ridiculed for his position on adding fluoride to our drinking water. Some moron actually painted a swastika on his garage door one night. This did not sway his resolve or opinion. Thank you Dr. Barrett wherever you may be.

Okay, now I'll confess: I have been a soda junkie all my life. In recent years my weight began to balloon. That got my attention! I began trying to eliminate certain foods and change my eating habits in order to reduce weight and also live a healthier life. I used to enjoy good (or even not so good) cream soda – black cherry and grape.

I couldn't seem to break the habit so finally one day I went to a hypnotist. I guess I was willing to try anything. I'm proud to say it's now been over two years without soda and still no cravings! Hypnotism doesn't work for everyone in every situation, but it sure worked for me in this one. By eliminating soda, I eliminated a few hundred pounds of sugar every year!

Potato chips are another junk food. Think about it this way: those chips are merely a medium to carry salt and grease. If you don't believe me, do this little experiment. Take a big potato chip and hold it with tweezers. Hold it over a plate and light it up. One chip will yield about ten disgusting drops of fat! Seriously, is that what you want to ingest?

Want a tasty, healthy alternative? A friend of mine taught me this trick. She made her own chips out of kale. Delicious! Most salsas aren't too bad. Be cautious to check the calorie and fat count in most dips.

And then there's ice cream and popcorn. Again, read the labels. Pay attention to the fat content and calorie counts.

Surprisingly, some nuts are really good, healthy snacks. It is best to enjoy them raw and unsalted.

So, let's review

If you're a TV junkie, you are severely restricting your chances of finding a wonderful BB woman. There is one out there and you could be the guy she is looking for. However, you won't find her if you're sitting at home, munching on junk food, and watching the boob tube.

C'mon! Get out there, present yourself well, and find her. It's like catching a butterfly. You can run around with a net, looking like a fool, or you can sit on a park bench and eventually one will land on your shoulder.

Hobbies

Hobbies are a great place to meet BB ladies. Stamp and coin collecting, art or pottery classes, photography, bird watching, and cooking classes are just a few ideas. Having a common hobby is a great way to spend time together. If you don't have a hobby, now's the time to start one!

Where to Meet Them

Being handy around the kitchen or being willing to try will endear you to the hearts (and taste buds) of many BB women. I have included some of my favorite recipes in the Appendix at the end of this book. They are simple and easy to prepare, fun to make, and require little cleanup!

Being handy in the kitchen also means you should be helping out with the table prep and cleanup. Having good table manners is an absolute requirement. This will be discussed further in Chapter 7 when we discuss manners.

Sports, both active and passive, are venues where BB women are involved. Some are more formal and strenuous than others. Attending college or professional games draws a lot of alumni and team groupies. Tennis, racquetball, pickleball, and badminton are great racquet sports. However, be careful. I have heard that couple's mixed doubles tennis has actually caused a few divorces!

Recently, coed touch flag football, coed softball, and coed no-dunk basketball have also become popular. Golf remains America's the #1 sport. Walking, bowling, bicycling, jogging, rowing, motorcycling, and gym exercise classes are examples of activities with millions of participants.

Concerning walking, there are those who walk for distance and those who walk for pleasure and serenity. If you are in the latter group, walk with a grandchild. Not only do you get the pride of showing off your beautiful family, but nearly all women are attracted to children. A secondary benefit to walking with a child is that women will think highly of you for your depth of love and commitment. You will also give that grandchild a lifetime of warm and fuzzies about the time they spent with grandpa.

Consider adopting a pet.

If you don't have a nearby grandchild, find a dog. I walk with a cute dog, but any dog will do. If you don't have a dog, borrow one from a friend or the local pet shelter. Dogs attract women, as well as the dog walker. It gives you an immediate subject or conversation and the ability to speak without any pressure or ulterior motive.

You can talk about the dog's breed, their history, the dog's personality, their veterinarian, other dogs you have parented, etc. You might even suggest walking together or meeting again. If your dog is friendly, bring them to the local dog park or pet friendly restaurants. It will be good therapy for the dog and an opportunity for you to meet a BB woman!

Did you know having a pet lengthens the life expectancy of senior citizens? If you are up to it, rescue a pet from the local humane society. Your pet will know that you rescued them and they will provide tremendous loyalty and happiness. At the Center for Spiritual Living in St. Augustine, Florida, Rev. Ken Wilcox once said, "Pets are your best spiritual partners."

I once saw a bumper sticker with a picture of a dog. It said, "Who rescued who?"

Think about it. You can leave your home in a bad mood or upset about something, even something the dog did. When you return, the dog conveys to you, "Hey, glad you're back. I missed you and I love you!" You rarely get that response from humans.

Todd was a friend of mine who rescued Buddy, a Rottweiler. Buddy was the center of attention wherever he went. At the dog park, the other dogs looked up to him as if he were the park protector.

Where to Meet Them

While at the dog park, Todd had an unusual habit. Instead of throwing a ball for Buddy to retrieve, Todd used chunks of raw meat! Buddy loved this game.

It was ironic that Buddy would run to retrieve the meat chunks because if you threw a tennis ball, he would ignore it and give you a truly condescending look as if to say, "Whaddya you think I am...*A DOG?*"

Buddy had been rescued and he was his pet parents' constant companion. He was so protective, he would sometimes trip people. He also invaded the king size bed in the middle of the night. He just knew – his comfort came first. Since he was around 125 pounds, he was a night time annoyance, but lovingly so.

Buddy's all time favorite enjoyment was to ride in the car. His pet parents couldn't say the word "ride" or even spell "r-i-d-e" without Buddy heading full speed to the front door. Generally, he stopped a little too late, causing many front door collisions.

Buddy's nails were wreaking havoc on the Mercedes upholstery, so the dad bought him his own car. It was a cheap SUV clunker, with lots of rust and a bad transmission that only moved in first gear. It was in Florida and at least it did have excellent air conditioning. They would lower the rear seat, start the SUV, and leave the air conditioning running at max. They would give him a bowl of water and Buddy was happy for many hours.

The really funny thing was when other dogs were being walked past him on the sidewalk, Buddy would rush to the back window and look at the other dogs with his best Andrew Dice Clay imitation, as if to say, "You gotta walk? On a leash? Heck, I've got my own car!"

BABY BOOMER WOMEN

It was Buddy's car and he knew it. Buddy had a tremendous spirit that would be difficult to duplicate.

Craig was another friend of mine. He built a custom home high up on a mountaintop. When his beautiful home was completed, he then built an exact replica for his beloved St. Bernard. It was to-scale, including framed out windows and doors, sprayed sheet rock ceilings, Formica walls (for easy cleaning), wall-to-wall carpeting with padding, and even an attached garage. When people looked at it in disbelief, Craig simply replied, "If the situation were reversed, the dog would do the same for me!" And the dog would have!

You probably noticed I used the term "pet parents" instead of "owner" or "master." I am the last guy to endorse political correctness but in this situation I think the term fits. Who else gives you perpetual, deep, unconditional love? As much as we may love our parents, mates, and children, there may be the rare or even occasional times when the love doesn't shine as brightly as it normally does. Not so with a dog. A dog's love is unconditional and constant. Where else can you find that?

As much as dogs are loved everywhere, your relationship with your potential partner's dog is important. What if the dog is not human friendly? What if your partner is so devoted to the dog that it is way over the top? What if the dog has other problems? Yes, dogs are great but the flip side is that it is a financial commitment and a huge parenting responsibility.

If you can accept the responsibility and have the space, time, and money to devote to a pet, do it! Being a pet parent will provide you with long-lasting companionship and happiness.

Where to Meet Them

Yoga may not be considered to be a sport by some, but it is an excellent way to relieve stress, tone the body, improve balance, and clear the mind. At one point in my life, I was a NCAA Division I ladies basketball coach. If I were to do it again, I would replace the strength and conditioning coach with a yoga instructor. It's hard to overstress the benefits of yoga.

I know, I know – most men aren't going to love this idea. At first. But, stay with me here. Did you know all yoga classes have more women than men? I have been to some yoga classes where I was the only guy in the room! With that ratio of women to men, well, you figure it out!

The gym is not only a place for physical and health improvement, but also a meeting place with great social interaction. At the gym you will be improving your health and appearance while being in the company of many BB ladies, who are probably there for the same reason. Sometimes people are at the gym for some rehab from surgery or an accident.

Be ready with some possible ways to open a conversation. You certainly don't want to start a conversation with, "Hi, I just had my appendix out." There are acceptable topics that are natural for the gym. For example, "Do you like the elliptical machine more than the stationary bike?"

A very important aspect is your eye contact. Many ladies at the gym wear tights and other figure revealing clothes while there. You must keep reminding yourself to keep your eyes focused on her face, not her body, no matter how appealing it may be. You don't want to make her feel uncomfortable because you got lazy with your eyes. This is basic manners!

I know a lady who works out regularly and has a very attractive shape... especially in tights. It's not like being covered by overcoats and bulky sweaters as is done in cold weather. Know what I mean, Vern? When she's working out at the gym and finds herself in a conversation that may lead to a dinner invitation, she asks the man to close his eyes. And then she asks him what color eyes she has. The correct answer gets the date and the loser goes back to the Gong Show!

Church, Coaching, and Concerts

Church is a tremendous place to meet a BB lady. You are already connected spiritually and there is a network of women who are share your spiritual principles. Even if there is not someone for you at your church, I am sure that someone in the congregation, or even the pastor, has a BB lady friend or relative who is available. Many churches have adult singles groups for socializing.

Grandchildren's activities are another avenue to discover the right lady. Youth ball games or recitals are great because they are no-pressure situations, yet there is commonality by simply attending those activities. Even better, consider volunteering to coach. Coaching a kid's team is a great opportunity to help kids and be a role model or mentor. When you give, you receive tenfold in return.

Concerts and performances of all kinds are filled with people who want to expand their lives and have an appreciation of the arts. Again the commonality of interests makes conversation easy.

Political and intellectual meetings

Political or intellectual meetings are also good places where many BB women donate their time. Please note that political and intellectual are completely different. You've heard the

Where to Meet Them

term "oxymoron," right? Like "military intelligence." Those two words are contradictory.

If you believe in one political party's general philosophy, go to their meetings or volunteer to work on a campaign. Intellectually, many colleges and libraries have guest speakers or exhibitions that may interest you. But "intellectual" is usually the opposite of "political."

I was once having a friendly conversation with a guy about some upcoming legislation. He was a retired engineer and appeared to be a pretty bright man. But then he flatly stated that if his party proposed the legislation then he would support it. However, if the other party proposed the exact same legislation, he would be against it. See what I mean? He was totally political with no real intellectual thought at all.

This is just another example of how blind party loyalty is destroying our country! We went on to discuss Palm Springs, California, where I once partnered in a business. I was telling him what a great place Palm Springs is. With absolutely fabulous, wonderful people, tremendous restaurants, and lively night life. Yes, the summer heat is a drawback. He really loved hearing that they have roads named after Gerald Ford and Ronald Reagan. But still, he couldn't change his negative perception of this beautiful place. Why? Because he had heard there was a large gay population there. I just shook my head and walked away. I have no time for shallow thinkers like this.

The internet: the good, the bad, and some help

By now we all know about internet dating. The internet has become an excellent tool in finding a potential mate. However, this is a double-edged sword. There are some great people out there but also tons of scammers, liars, and jerks. Keep your eyes wide open.

I say this from experience. I have been on the internet and have met some fabulous women there, but also more than my share of scammers, liars, and jerks.

Some people do not go on the internet because they never learned how to safely navigate online. C'mon, if you can't use a computer by this time, you probably still believe in the flat earth theory or creationism. Maybe it's time to take a class! Or find a friend (or grandchild) to help you.

Others may not go on a dating site because they think most of the members are losers. This simply is not true. For a variety of reasons, there are a number of quality people on dating websites but yes, you have to filter through them to find the right one. It's not much different than meeting a new person in a bar, at a softball game, or at a dance. At first, you don't know anything about them. It takes time. Of course, some are lying! They're people, remember?

So, be smart. Don't trust anyone at the very beginning. It doesn't matter if you met online or in person. The concepts are the same.

On the dating sites, you create your own profile first. You describe who you are and what you are looking for in a potential relationship. Here are some suggested do's and don'ts concerning computer dating tips. These apply for either gender.

On your profile, use only current pictures. If you do use an older picture, be sure you tell your readers the year it was taken. Casual, amateur pictures are best. Glamour photos look pretentious and will only attract people looking for glamour rather than substance. Your photos should include at least a

Where to Meet Them

few good head shots and some that show your general physique and body structure. Action shots work well because they also convey activities you enjoy. A picture of you on the tennis court, a dance floor, or on a motorcycle lets everyone know what you love to do.

Photos should be honest and appealing but you don't want to portray yourself as a movie star type or more than what you actually are. Choose pictures that show your best assets and confidence in yourself. The more pictures, the better. Try for at least eight to ten. It's sometimes okay to post pictures that include your family, motorcycle, pet, boat, or car, just don't do it in such a way that you end up looking like you're bragging. Too much is just overwhelming.

One guy had his picture taken in front of a Ferrari and a Lear Jet. Unfortunately, he owned neither! Assuming he met a great gal, how do you think it will go when she finds out these pictures don't even come close to who he really is? He'll end up looking like a fraud.

The real owner of that Lear Jet eventually found out about this fraudulent picture and threatened legal action, forcing the guy to remove the picture of the Lear from his business cards.

Do not include artsy pictures of sunsets, etc. unless you are in them. Everyone knows you love your grandchildren or your pets, but the pictures should be about you, not about your family or your worldly assets. There will be time for that later.

Then it's time to write some paragraphs to describe who you are. Write truthfully about yourself and what you are truly looking for. (Sister Miriam Clare, my sixth grade teacher, would scold me for ending a sentence in a preposition! Fortunately, this Latin-based rule has finally bit the dust.)

Consider your online profile to be your resume for a possible romantic encounter! Just be truthful about who you are and what you want. This is not the time to be shy, nor is it time to brag or be unrealistic either. It's up to you.

If you're sixty, overweight, unkempt, bald, and looking for a twenty-five-year-old starlet... wake up, dude! Yes, you will get some responses but stop for just a minute. I'll give you three guesses about what they may be after.

Truthfulness is one of the basic requirements for a lasting relationship. If you are stumped as to what to write, go to one of your computer-savvy friends and ask for help. For starters, go back to your personal assessment of who you are and who you are looking for as described in the previous chapter.

So, let's assume you get this far. Your online profile is up and running with several photos. Be ready for the next step. You will probably start getting inquiries from women. This is where I want you to really pay attention. I'm about to give you some really good advice. Ready? Are you paying attention? Okay, here goes...

> *Be cautious!*

Be cautious! I might want to say it again. You know, just in case you were sleeping for a minute.

Be very cautious!

Why am I leaning on this point? Because there are so many stories about people falling for scams. You do NOT want to be one of those. So, keep reading. Here's rule #1:

Where to Meet Them

> *Internet Dating Rule #1:* *Do not answer unless there is a current picture from the person responding to your profile.*

If there is no picture, there is a reason. Troy was new at internet dating. He was looking forward to what might happen. It didn't take long before a woman responded to his profile. There was only one problem: She had no picture.

She said it was because she didn't have anything current. So, Troy asked if she could give him a description of herself. She agreed and said she looked like Joey Heatherton. Well! That certainly worked for him! He was pretty pumped up and couldn't wait to meet her in person.

The day came to meet. Troy walked in to the coffee shop happy and excited. His date? Well, let's just say she did look like Joey Heatherton in a sense. *Joey Hetherton's bulldog!* Can you imagine Troy's shock? How did this woman expect to start any kind of relationship when it all started with a lie?

Ready for Jay's Rule #2? This one's important too.

> *Internet Dating Rule #2:* *NEVER meet someone for the first time anywhere except a very public place.*

This is a basic security issue. NEVER meet someone for the first time anyplace other than a public place. First of all, you want it to be someplace easy to find, but more importantly, it should be a public place where there are lots of people. Women may be more tuned in to this rule, but men need to pay attention too. Scammers are everywhere.

Be aware of what the person says and also of the questions they ask. If something doesn't sound right to you, ask questions. If something is just not clear, ask!

Remember this too: First impressions can be misleading. Don't get too emotionally involved until you know each other. There's no substitute for time.

Remember serial killer Ted Bundy? He was said to be quite a charming individual.

Just take time and verify everything you're told. There are some really great people online but an equal number of liars, scammers, jerks, and swindlers.

I once knew of a lovely BB lady who met a guy online and very quickly fell in love with him. Only later did she discover that he was insanely deep into bizarre political writings, one of which was to urge citizens to shoot police officers!

Moral of the story? *Don't fall too fast.*

Okay, it's time for Jay's Rule #3.

> *Internet Dating Rule #3: Never send money to someone you haven't yet met in person.*

Sherry was a lovely lady who met Carl online. Carl was a very successful businessman who told Sherry he was building a bridge in Indonesia at the time. The two of them carried on via the internet for a while. Carl was absolutely charming. He once sent her 100 roses for no reason at all. Such a romantic gesture was very endearing to Sherry.

One day during their online messaging, Carl said "red tape" in Indonesia was holding up his business. He sounded really frustrated as he told her the business would be three days late in making a payment to him. Sounding a bit sheepish, he finally asked if she could loan him $14,000 for just three days. He said he needed it so he could make payroll.

I'm glad to tell you, Sherry wasn't that stupid. Many others are. Stories just like this are playing out every day. It's easy to get duped.

You may have seen some daytime TV shows where scammers and swindlers have been exposed. Some of the victims still refuse to admit the truth, even after they are presented with concrete, undisputable evidence. I'm sure it's embarrassing to know you fell for a scam. Some of the victims are normal people who fell for a dream and they can't seem to let it go.

Real life stories can open your eyes, so I want to tell you one more. Sheila was a classy BB lady who met Bill online. The two started an arrangement, which is different from a relationship. Bill told her what a successful professional he was and bragged that his retirement income was $80,000 a year. Little did he know that Sheila was worth well over eight figures. Do you think Sheila was impressed by Bill's five-figure income?

Thinking he would impress her, he took her to his mountain property and later to his beach home. Some time after that, she discovered the truth. Bill was nothing more than a low level civil service administrator. All those assets were actually from his deceased wife and his parent's estate.

Somebody should write a book about internet stories and dating. I am sure it would be very interesting.

The best story
I've saved the best for last. I want to tell you what I think is the all-time best internet dating story.

BABY BOOMER WOMEN

Wayne just happened to meet Diana, while waiting in line at a take-out Chinese restaurant. Wayne was a widower and Diana was separated and in the process of divorce. Eventually, she completed the divorce and the two of them married. After just a few happy years, Diana passed away.

Wayne eventually was ready to move on. He went on an internet dating site and after several dates (some good and some not so good), he made a connection with Andrea, a BB lady who lived 1,200 miles away. Andrea was living in a large northern city and Wayne lived in Florida.

However, Andrea said that her dad had lived in Florida, but had recently passed away. She planned to sell her business up north, move to Florida, and reunite with her mom and extended family. She had been on the internet dating site for a year but had met only one guy whom she had dated for a short time.

Andrea had a striking appearance, was a great communicator, possessed a terrific sense of humor, and was self-sufficient financially. She also said that during her year on the dating site, she had received 6,500 hits on her profile, which he was later able to verify. She described all of those 6,500 hits as coming from "frogs." In her typical straight-forward communication style, she explained. She wasn't looking for frogs; she was looking for a Prince.

After much communication with several different men, Andrea eventually narrowed it down to two men from Florida. She made plans to go on trial dates with each of them when she arrived in Florida.

She dated guy #1 a couple of times. It went well and they continued to call and text daily.

About a week later she met Wayne (guy #2) and they hit it off immediately. On their first date, Wayne and Andrea went to an informal seaside restaurant for lunch. They chatted easily on the way in casual, comfortable conversation. Oddly, Andrea began to ask about Wayne's deceased wife (Diana). Where was she from? Where did Diana's ex live? Did they have children? Where did the children live? What was Diana's occupation, and so forth?

When Wayne and Andrea got to the restaurant she turned mysteriously gloomy and secretive. It was an oceanfront seafood kind of place and Wayne began to wonder if she might have been offended about something. Maybe she wanted to go to a nicer restaurant. He offered to leave but she was still very reserved. So they stayed and enjoyed the fresh seafood.

The date continued when Wayne invited her to his home, where they enjoyed a casual game of Scrabble. As evening approached, they went for a walk on the beach, dinner at a nicer restaurant, dancing at two different places, and finally concluded the evening with a slight kiss and a warm hug at 3:00 AM!

Early the next day, he contacted her and they met several times over the next week or so. In no time, Wayne took over and guy #1 was out of the picture.

Fast forward a few months and Wayne and Andrea are now forming a warm and wonderful relationship.

One balmy Sunday afternoon, they were enjoying a glass of wine in the hot tub when out of the blue Andrea said to him, "Do you remember I moved here from 1,200 miles away?"

"Yep," he responded.

"And do you remember that I had 6,500 responses from the internet dating site?"

"Yes, I do," he said. "You showed me the response count on your computer."

BABY BOOMER WOMEN

"And do you remember that I picked out two men I wanted to meet when I got here?"

"Yes, I do. I was one of the lucky ones, the one who you chose."

"Well," she said, "the first guy..."

Not sure he wanted to hear what might be coming, he interrupted her. "Hey, whatever happened is in the past. I have no worries about it because you are here with me now and that's all that matters to me."

They fell silent in the pleasures of wine and warm water. She let the thoughts roll through her mind until about fifteen minutes later, she tried again. "So you remember the 1,200 miles, the 6,500 guys and the two I picked?"

Not sure where this was going, Wayne said, "Listen, we've been over this before and as long as the guy didn't molest you or beat you, it's yesterday's news as far as I am concerned. It's just not an issue for me. No worries!" That seemed to satisfy her.

Until... another half hour and another glass of wine. Apparently, she was not done. She started again, trying to make some headway. "Well, about that other guy..."

Now he was getting irritated. "Obviously you've got something major to say, so say it. Just remember that no matter what you say, I love you and I want our relationship to continue to grow and flourish." Maybe she was going to lay a verbal "Dear John" on him. Now he was getting nervous.

"Well, just in case we bump into him somewhere, someday..." She paused long enough to take a really deep breath. "I just wanted you to know that the other guy was (are you ready for this?)... DIANA'S FIRST HUSBAND!"

Diana's first husband? His deceased first wife's husband? It took a few minutes for this to sink in.

YIKES!

Can you spell S-H-O-C-K?

What are the odds of moving 1,200 miles, picking out two random men out of a group of 6,500 and learning that each of them had been married at different times to the same woman? *To his Diana?*

Even the Twilight Zone's Rod Serling couldn't write that script!

Eventually, after the shock began to wear off, he put the pieces together. During the drive on that very first date, as she asked those questions about Wayne's deceased wife Diana, Andrea was able to connect the dots. She figured out that both of her dates had been married at different times to the same woman – Diana. Wow!

Wayne and Andrea eventually became engaged, but some time later broke up only to become engaged again. Unfortunately, she was anxious to get married and he was hesitant. Ultimately, she left him and eventually married someone else.

Everybody comes through your life for a reason.

If you have a weirder internet story than this, I'd love to hear it!

I saved the best idea for last!

I have saved the best way to meet a BB woman for last. Hear me out on this as some of you may not initially agree. Just stay with me. After reading this explanation, it should be clear to you.

The absolute best way to meet a BB woman is through DANCING!

Think of it. Where can you introduce yourself to a complete stranger, hold her in your arms for about four minutes, talk about whatever stuff you want while she can't get away, and afterward she thanks you for it. Can you imagine going up to a complete stranger in a supermarket and holding her in your arms in a dancing position? The police would be taking you out in handcuffs for being a pervert! However, in a dance setting, it's not only acceptable, it's expected!

Dancing is GREAT! This has been said before and based on my experience, it is true. Dancing is the connection between body and soul! I realize some may claim to be too shy, or say they have no rhythm, or they have two left feet. I've heard it all. But, they're all just excuses.

A wonderful instructor and friend Michael Kielbasa once told me, "There are two kinds of dancers, those who dance to express and those who dance to impress...and the latter usually don't!"

Now here's the truth: There is some kind of dancing that fits everyone.

Obviously, every type of dance has starter, intermediate, and advanced dancers. I can assure you that any type of dance has friendly people who will help you learn their particular kind of dancing and help you improve. Many types of dancing have group lessons before the actual dancing event.

You can find professional dance instructors that offer group classes. If you prefer, you can take individual instruction. Group classes are more affordable, but it's your choice. Help is available for anyone who feels awkward or think they have absolutely no dancing ability.

Where to Meet Them

If you find yourself resisting this whole idea, I'm asking you to bear with me on this. I know this world. I've heard the stories. There are scores of BB women who told me they used to dance with their husbands or boyfriends, but for whatever reason, they didn't dance together any longer. When we were all younger, dancing was a prelude to a fertility rite. Later in life, some men thought they were going to get lucky when they went home anyway, so why dance?

Well now, you're back in the dating scene and the world has changed. Dancing is no longer a prelude to intimacy. Have you ever gone to a wedding and seen the women out on the dance floor dancing with each other? Many times their boring husbands or boyfriends are sitting there, getting drunk or talking about some brainless sports statistic.

Go out and dance! It's great fun and in short order you'll discover for yourself this best-kept-secret: Dancing is a great non-pressure way to met happy BB women. I say "happy," because if you go to a casual dance, almost everyone on the dance floor is smiling! Dancing can be enjoyed at local informal venues or at professional competition events.

Okay, I'm game! Where do I start?

Start with the type of music you like. If you're a country music kind of guy, you'll probably enjoy country two-step dancing. If you really love classical music, you might start with ballroom dancing. Those who prefer Latin music would be best suited for the Latin dances. People who enjoy R&B, funk, pop, or soul music would tend to gravitate toward swing dancing. Many ethnic groups enjoy dancing from their homelands too. Each type of music has a few styles of dancing. I'll explain some of the more common ones.

Square dancing is fun and a great way to meet friendly people. It's not overly complicated for beginners, it's relatively easy to learn, and can be enjoyed by almost anyone, especially at the beginner level. There are square dancing groups in most areas. Square dancing is great for those who claim to have two left feet. The square dance caller actually tells you what to do! The music is usually specific to each dance but generally it has its roots in country music. The dance attire is definitely western.

Ballroom dancing includes many types of dances and some are more difficult to learn than others. The more popular ballroom dances include the foxtrot, waltz, rumba, cha-cha, and tango. The music tends to be more classical in nature, except for the cha-cha and rumba where the Latin music takes over. Ballroom dancing is sometimes more rigid and exacting than other types of dances. The dress at competitions is definitely more formal than at venues for other dances.

Latin dancing includes many types of dances because it is deeply rooted in all Latin countries, including Spain, the Caribbean, Central America, and South America. Popular Latin dances include the salsa, cha-cha, bolero, bachata, meringue, mambo, paso doble, samba, and others. Each dance has its own distinct footwork pattern and is performed to different music tempos. Latin dancers usually dress informally, often with a Latin urban influence. Salsa is probably one of the most popular dances worldwide.

Country dancing includes line dances (there are hundreds of different line dances), country two-step, cowboy cha-cha (also known as traveling cha-cha), among others. Attire at country dances is definitely boots and cowboy hats, although basic jeans or other informal dress is fine, and the music will be country western music.

Ethnic dances are native dances for people from various countries. These dances include the Polish (Slavic) polka, the Italian tarantella, the Russian kozachok, Greek bouzouki dancing, Middle Eastern belly dancing, and others. There is probably a native dance associated with every country worldwide.

There are many types of other dances, including ballet, tap, point, jazz, break dancing, limbo, margarita, and pole dancing, to name a few. Unless it was for a goofy joke, I would not recommend pole dancing to any BB man. It would probably not be a sensual sight to witness.

Swing dancing

In my opinion, swing dancing is the most enjoyable. This broad category includes the lindy hop, hustle, shag beach dancing, American Bandstand bop, and east coast swing. Newer dances also in this broad category include the night club two-step and west coast swing.

The lindy hop is the one most closely aligned with the once popular jitterbug dance from the 1940s. Lindy hop dancers will often have guys throw gals over their heads, around their shoulders, and through their legs. It is definitely an up tempo dance and is wonderful to watch, but I wouldn't recommend it for BB men or BB women. Why? Well, yes, it's a lot of fun, but for BB dancers (with less strength and thinner bones) you have to face the possibility of falls and broken bones, especially during the learning stage.

The hustle is closely associated with the disco era. Watch the movies *Staying Alive* or *Saturday Night Fever* and watch John Travolta do his thing.

Night club two is a dance that combines gracefulness with a hint of sensuality. It is basically the slow dance played at swing dances. It was invented in 1965 by then 15-year-old Buddy Schwimmer. His children, Lacey and Benji, have both been featured on national TV dance shows dancing the elegant night club two.

There are four basic types of swing dances that are popular today: bop, east coast swing, shag, and west coast swing.

Bop dancing was what we watched on Dick Clark's *American Bandstand* when we were teenagers. It's basically a couple's dance where each partner is equal and is performed in a non-confined circular type of motion. The timing is at least 130 beats per minute and the foot pattern is one-two-three, one-two-three, one-two.

East coast swing is similar but a little more flamboyant. It has the same footwork and the same tempo. Both are pretty fast dances and are the updated versions of the 40s jitterbug.

The shag and west coast swing are similar in nature. The tempo of both dances generally ranges from about 100 to 125 beats per minute. They are different from the bop and east coast in a couple of ways. The bop and east coast are danced in a non-confined area, sometimes in a circle. The shag and west coast are considered to be track dances.

Much of the early shag dancing was done on a beach, with a beach towel used as a dance floor. Since the west coast is a cousin of the shag, both dances are performed on an imaginary railroad track. The wood cross members are called the track; the steel rails are called the rails. Both are danced in a back and forth motion as if on railroad tracks; one partner has to get off the tracks and on to either rail for the other partner to pass by them.

The shag is considered to be a man's dance because the man is the dominant featured dancer. He is more of the show

Where to Meet Them

of the dance and generally she allows him to do his moves. West coast is considered to be a ladies' dance because generally she is the focal point of the dance. In west coast, the man's job as leader is to make the lady look good as she follows his lead. He puts her through the different moves while they dance.

The shag was invented in the 1920s somewhere between the Charleston and the Big Apple dances. The man is the focal point of the shag. When first introduced, it was considered to be too sexually flamboyant and was somewhat dormant for several years. It was eventually resurrected in the early 50s around the time Elvis arrived on the national music scene. With Elvis' stage gyrations, the shag was no longer considered overly suggestive.

The original home of the shag is in North Myrtle Beach, South Carolina. South Carolina is one of only two states with an official state dance and, you guessed it, the Shag is the official state dance! Four times a year, North Myrtle Beach holds an unbelievable shag extravaganza called SOS. People shag dance on the beach, at bars, on the streets, on sidewalks, and everywhere shag beach music can be heard! Thousands attend and it is truly a sight to behold. Beach type music is considered to be the best music for shagging.

I once knew a flight attendant whose regular run was from Atlanta to London. As a member of the Atlanta Shag Club, she danced at several shag venues in the Atlanta area.

One day she was going through London's Heathrow Airport with her luggage and she noticed that people were looking at her strangely and even pointing fingers at her. She thought maybe her slip was showing or maybe she had a rip in her panty hose. She was a little confused but when she unpacked her bags at the hotel it all made embarrassing sense. One of her shoulder bags had her club monogram saying

"Atlanta Shag Club." Slowly, it dawned on her. Shagging in the UK has a different meaning than shag dancing in the USA. As Austin Powers would say, "Shag me baby!"

Whoops!

Although there are some who dispute this, Buddy Schwimmer is generally credited for inventing west coast swing. But no one disputes that it was he who promoted it to the popular worldwide dance that it is today. In my opinion, west coast swing is the best dance around. It is a little more difficult to learn, but once you catch on it is a tremendously fun dance.

Some experienced dancers have trouble learning west coast swing for a few reasons. First, on the one count, the leader (man) steps backward with his left foot as opposed to most other dances where the leader goes forward on the one count. Secondly, west coast is a six count dance: one-two, three and four, five and six. It also has a move called the Whip where the foot work goes to an eight count.

There is another common move called the Play where the follower (lady) can extend the foot count to a ten, twelve (or more) footwork count. A great thing about west coast is that west coasters are always smiling on the dance floor, nobody is critical of one's ability, the attire is casual, and it is danced to happy music – R&B, funk, soul, and pop.

Google "west coast swing." You'll find beginner lessons nearly everywhere. Give it a try! Later, click on some exhibitions and you will see how incredible the professional west coasters perform. They are simply amazing. It's not only fun to dance, but amazing to watch.

California is the other state with an official state dance. Want to guess what it is? Yep! It's the west coast swing.

Where to Meet Them

I have had the honor of dancing with nationally ranked professional west coast dancers in San Diego, Palm Springs, Redlands, and San Francisco, California as well as Orlando, Tampa, and Daytona Beach, Florida. I confess it makes me a little nervous to dance with a dancer with that incredibly superior ability. But as a true professional, they dance at my level and they always compliment me on my continuing progress as a dancer. That means a lot. These are the things that exemplify what the west coast dance community is about.

What's not to love?

I once attended a major shag affair with several hundred dancers. It was held in the grand ballroom of a major hotel. As part of the demonstrations, there was an exhibition of the differences between shag, east coast, and west coast dances.

The shag participant was the winner of the National Shag competition. In other words, he was the number one shagger in America! He danced with his regular shag partner.

The east coast participant placed second in the National East Coast contest and he danced with his regular east coast partner.

The west coast participant was Mark Traynor, a well-known instructor from Orlando who danced with Annie Mariani.

Annie was a competent dancer, but she was not his regular dance partner. The DJ played a great tune and after a few seconds all eyes were glued to the west coast dancers. An unranked west coast instructor with an unfamiliar partner clearly out-danced the #1 shagger in America, and the #2 east coaster, both of whom were dancing with their regular dance partners! Quite a show, indeed!

I had a good friend who was short, bald, and not especially handsome. At weddings, he made it a habit to ask the bride's or groom's grandmother for a dance. All the young ladies would notice that and I am sure they were thinking what a nice guy he was.

He knew exactly what he was doing. He had learned the magic of dancing! While he was the perfect gentleman, dancing with the grandmothers, he was also checking out all the women watching him dance. Those were the women he then asked to dance later in the evening.

All I can say is I never saw him leave a wedding alone! He usually ended up taking one of the bridesmaids with him due to his dancing!

My first wife used to say, "You know who is a great dancer? Any guy who gets on the floor and tries!"

As much as I love swing dancing and the socialization of mature dancing, I've seen men make some crazy mistakes on the dance floor.

Jack is a retired telephone company executive. He's got a fat retirement; he's nice looking with a trim body; he has a good sense of humor, and good manners. Pretty much has the whole package.

However, when Jack goes to dances, he's like a shark after new meat. He finds a complete stranger, asks her to dance, and proceeds to grab her tightly – very tightly against his body. This is belly and boob grinding at its worst. Several women have actually walked off the floor halfway through the dance! Others have finished the dance but then simply refused to dance with him again. Due to his friendly, boyish personality, he does get away with it occasionally.

Apparently, Jack is so blind, he doesn't seem to get it. He could mix very well with many women but he has given himself the reputation of a letch. If he simply behaved himself on the

Where to Meet Them

dance floor, many women would be willing to consider a relationship with him. He has ruined it for himself!

If you are serious about finding a wonderful BB lady, get on the dance floor!

5
That First Introduction

So, you've read this far and you think you're ready. You decide where you're going to go to find some BB women. Once there, it will be time to walk up and start a conversation. Are you ready for that?

Wherever it is, there are some guidelines to help you out. You only get one chance to make that all-important first impression, so let's make it good! I want you to have some likelihood of success.

What will you say?

There are general topics such as work, sports, college, hobbies, kids, grandkids, and many more where a light conversation will work easily. And "light" is what you want, especially at first.

Some of this is dependent on the surroundings. A first conversation at church will probably be different from one that may occur at a cocktail party. *Did you enjoy the pastor's discussion this morning?* That's very certainly different than *Do you know the party's host from work or other activities?*

One thing is certain. All BB women have been hit upon before, most of them throughout their lifetimes. Do not ever attempt to initially approach a BB woman with some stupid pick-up line. They will see through that immediately and you will appear to be either a fool or a jerk.

What may have been a great ice-breaker in previous years simply will not work today. The only way a pick-up line might work is if you make a joke out of it. You might say, "If we were single and in our 20s, I'd say something like blah, blah, blah." Or, "With your great looks (or some other compliment), I would be willing to bet you have heard every pick-up line ever invented, so I won't insult you by trying something as juvenile as that with a lady like you. By the way, what were the best and worst ones you've ever heard?"

That being said, there are some unique ways to start a conversation without it sounding like a pick-up line. If you're in a bar or a club you might approach a lady who is a complete stranger and ask, "Are you hitting on me?" A friend of mine uses this approach and it works for him.

Usually the woman is bewildered and responds, "No, I'm not."

He then says, "Are you sure you're not hitting on me?"

By this time the answer is more firm. "No, I'm not!"

His ready reply is, "Well, if you'd dance with me (have dinner with me, etc.), you might change your mind."

If you have something creative, you might try it but be careful.

Never forget that all BB women have been through this drill many times so don't make the mistake of thinking you'll be able to con any of them. Honesty and sincerity are the key concepts here.

Ask a question!

If you want to start a conversation, don't just state a fact. Asking a question is better because it invites a response. Even if you don't get a response, it's not necessarily a dead issue, although it's not a good sign. You may try another way to break the ice, but if there does not seem to be any connection, do not force the issue. You never know. For whatever reason, she may not be interested in you, but she may know of someone who might be. Never forget the importance of networking. It can happen successfully in the strangest and most unexpected ways.

If you do get a response, follow up on her reply; don't change the subject or just drop it. Try to develop a conversation where both parties have something to say. The key elements here are to listen to what she has to say and maintain eye contact. Don't look like an idiot by looking around the room while trying to carry on a conversation with her. Your eye contact is important because it shows respect for her. You're focused on her, not anyone else. Be careful not to let your eyes wander to her body, regardless of how appealing it may be.

Listen and show sincere interest in whatever she has to say. Initially keep it vanilla and light. If it's working well, there will be plenty of time for in-depth conversations on more complex subjects in the future. This is not the time or place for discussions about religion, politics, deep social issues, etc. (unless you are at church, a political meeting, or a venue where that subject matter might come up naturally).

Generally, keep the subject matter light. You may do well here to ask some superficial issues. Ask questions about her but equally important, remember her answers. If you ask if she attended college, remember which one. If you ask her occupation, remember the answer. Then follow up with that new information. "I knew somebody who went to that college." Or, "How did your occupational requirements change throughout your working years?"

We are all different. Everyone has their own approach to this, but here are a few general tips about that all-important opening introduction.

That First Introduction

Most importantly smile and be friendly! Present yourself as confident but not egotistical or pushy. Be yourself, know who you are, be proud of that, and act accordingly.

This is not the time to be shy or the strong silent type. That only works in the movies. I recall seeing a chick flick several years ago where Julia Roberts had a mad crush on a guy and he was too shy to pick up on it. Obviously it was a movie. Any man who would not accept Julia Robert's affection should forfeit his man card!

One of the "C" words – communication – is the key element here. This is critically important because if the relationship develops, good communication skills will thwart any potential arguments.

BB women are attracted to confident men but not if the man appears to be conceited or self-absorbed. To prove this point, do the following with a BB woman who is not a potential girlfriend. Find a BB lady who is a relative, gal pal, or the like. Go to the mall, park, or any public place and ask her to rate the BB men who pass by. Ask her to assign each man a number on a scale from 1 to 10.

Many BB men will have sagging, ugly beer bellies and they automatically put themselves out of any kind of serious contention. What BB lady wants to be with a guy who cares so little about himself, or is so addicted to alcohol or tobacco they allow themselves to decline to that type of physical appearance?

Out of the remaining ones, some will be better looking than others, some will be dressed well, some carry themselves well, and some are just generally more attractive than others. Odds are the one she gives the highest number to will not be any of these. Are you surprised?

BABY BOOMER WOMEN

Here's the point: women are not like men! I assume you already knew this! The most obvious difference is that whenever there are two or more of them together, women go to the restroom in pairs! Conversely, men possess the ability to pee solo.

There are intangibles that women sense intuitively while considering a man. A man may have better posture or mannerisms that set him apart from the rest. The way he carries himself, the sparkle in his eyes, the depth of the way he observes things are just a few things women sense better than men. Trust me on this: She will not always choose the best looking or best dressed. Those guys could very well lose out to the guy who has those intangibles.

The same is true when observing BB women in a public places. Granted, men are more visual than women and typically more lustful. Many men will just look at a lady's face and body and end it there. However, more astute lady watchers will be more in tune to their walk, the way they carry themselves, and their sensuality. Sensuality is one of those intangibles not dependent on facial or body features.

Remember the old story about the movie producer who got the young, beautiful, incredibly sexy starlet into bed? The only way he could determine if she had an orgasm was when she dropped her emery board during intimacy. Filing her nails was more important to her than being an active sex partner!

Did you know there are women who can't walk past a mirror without stopping to admire themselves? There are also women who are fanatics about plucking their eyebrows (ouch!). Some continuously fidget with their long hair, apparently thinking it is sexy. In reality, they are probably erotic duds.

By the way, have you ever heard a guy talk about a first date when he raved on and on about what a great set of eyebrows a lady had? I can assure you that when it comes to sets of things on a lady's body, eyebrows are not the first things being noticed and mentioned!

About women's hair

I want you to think about long hair on BB women. As we age, our hair deteriorates just like the rest of our bodies. Some BB women are so consumed by the Hollywood look and the glamour magazines, they feel they have to retain that long hair look.

But maybe some of them are still trying to relive their cheerleader days from high school. That long hair feeds their delusion. Imagine BB men who are still wearing crew cuts (assuming they have any hair left). The BB men who still want long hair on their lady may be subconsciously still trying to score the cheerleader from fifty years ago.

I personally feel that BB women with shoulder length or shorter hair are more attractive and stylish than the women who try to maintain the cheerleader, longer hair look. A BB lady with shorter styled hair shows more natural self-confidence. She's comfortable and looks more modern and stylish than BB women still wearing long hair. It also changes the relative geometry of her face and often the neckline and ears display her face in a more provocative manner. Additionally the vertical lines of long hair accentuates any age lines the lady may have on her face.

Shorter hair is easier to maintain and is less of an obstruction during intimacy. If your lady is adamant about keeping long hair, ask her to wear it up or back occasionally. Wearing a bun, French twist, or a single braid can alter a lady's appearance dramatically. There are tons of styles where long hair is worn up or back. The idea is to get it off her face.

BABY BOOMER WOMEN

It's also a good opportunity for a compliment. Your face is so pretty, why hide it with your hair?

Another way of working around the short hair issue is to offer to buy her a wig or two, just to cover up a bad hair day. It will also allow her to be playful and change her appearance occasionally. Different colors and styles can change a lady's looks dramatically. I have known BB men who have bought wigs for their ladies to be used in harmless role playing. I have also known BB women who wear wigs occasionally at functions, which will usually evoke comments from both genders.

Here is bit of history about short hair. After World War II, in the countries that had been occupied by the Nazis, there was a punishment for women who slept with the Nazi occupiers. They were considered to be traitors so in an effort to readily identify them, their heads were forcibly shaved. I understand that it takes at least five years to grow a full head of hair back after being shaved, so during those five years, they were easily recognized and pretty much ostracized.

In the mid 1950s the "Italian Cut" was introduced. This was a shorter style and it eliminated the stigma of wearing short hair. I understand it was popularized by the Italian actress Gina Lollobrigida.

You may remember a hilarious *I Love Lucy* episode where Lucy wanted to get an Italian cut but macho Ricky adamantly forbid it. To circumvent Ricky's orders, Lucy bought an Italian Cut wig. It was a great scene when Ricky thought Lucy had actually cut her hair. Completely astonished, he screamed, "Ah, Chihuahua Lucy! You look like a boy!" What great, wholesome humor!

There is an exception to the short hair preference. I call it the "Given Ups." These are women whose mates have lost interest in them for whatever reason and they just don't feel attractive or loved anymore. Consequently, they wear clothes that are not becoming and a basic, no-frills short haircut. From head to toe, they are not stylish. They just want something easy to maintain regardless of the look…very sad!

Incidentally, compliments should be often, truthful, sincere, and given in a warm, loving manner. BB women can filter the untrue comments very quickly, so don't ever attempt to use a fake line or a flimsy compliment as a way to get out of an apology after a bad word or an uncomfortable situation. Wrong! Never try to compliment your way out of an argument!

There is always something for which you can compliment her. Think about her many kind actions and words, her many accomplishments, or the wonderful things she adds to the relationship and to your life.

Remember the old saying, "There is always, always, always something to be happy about today." I have a sign on my computer: "Begin and end each day with a grateful heart."

6
Communication and Conversations

Some of us are just better than others when it comes to starting and sustaining a conversation. If you feel comfortable in chatting, then go ahead and do so. Remember that you are not talking with a long time friend who may accept certain out-of-the-way phrases or innuendo, so try to keep it pretty vanilla at the beginning. Things that may be slightly off color might be tolerated in the future but now is not that time. LISTEN when the BB lady speaks. Digest what she says and try to remember it for future comments or conversational topics.

Did she play a musical instrument or team sports in high school? Sometime in the future, that will be a great topic of conversation. Do you like this particular song or artist? Do you prefer professional sports, college sports, or the Olympics? Always keep in mind that it's about her, not you.

Yes, your comments are just as important as hers, but LISTENING will get you a lot further than talking. In the course of a conversation, if you are speaking about yourself, your history, or accomplishments, don't make it sound like you are bragging. Be low key about yourself and be willing to adapt to her style.

John was an ex-sailor who used to revert to his old Navy slang a lot. He would refer to his nose as his "Snot Locker." His BB lady didn't appreciate that term at all, but he continued to use it just to tease her. WRONG! John was completely insensitive to her and refused to adapt to her simple wishes. Don't make that mistake.

Communication and Conversations

I have known men who tried to impress women with (of all things) their car! One guy's opening line was always, "Wanna see my car?" Yes, it does impress women, but not in a positive way! One gal described him as a showy jerk.

One guy I knew was over-the-top politically weird. Not right or left, just bizarre.

Randy wanted to be married. He actually set a definite timetable for marriage, but get this: He already has a diamond ring picked for his yet-unknown bride. When asked why, Randy just shrugged his shoulders and said, "Every woman wants a diamond." I guess he thinks he's still in some long-ago century.

And then there's Sean. Sean just dives right in to sexuality and deeply feminine sexual responses.

Curtis brags about the beautiful women he has met online. He actually photographs them on the first date in order to show everyone the beauty of the women he dates. Imagine photographing a lady on the first date? When asked if he got a second date with any of them, he simply didn't answer. Maybe that's because Curtis doesn't get second dates.

Be selective in your conversational topics. Learn from the mistakes of the men in these stories.

Watch your language!

The use of the f-bomb is a huge mistake. By this time, every BB woman has heard it at least a million times. We all know the variety of stories of the origination of that word. Until and unless you hear it FROM HER in anger or for emphasis, do NOT use it. If by chance you slip sometime, profusely apologize immediately. It may make no difference to some women, but to others it is a major no-no.

Sam used the f-bomb in front of his best friend's new girlfriend all the time. Although he had been asked numerous times to stop, he just continued using this profanity. His friend explained to Sam that his profanity was disrespectful to his new girlfriend. But Sam refused. He just brushed it off with a sheepish "Sorry."

This pattern continued unchanged, which showed a total lack of respect for the girlfriend. Eventually this long-time friendship between the two guys ended. The guy got tired of Sam's disrespect of his girlfriend.

One European couple from our parent's generation was nearly derailed by the husband's indiscriminate use of this profanity. Finally, the wife sternly and truthfully told her husband that if he ever used the f-bomb again, she would divorce him.

Marriage saved!

If you can adapt, use freakin' or friggin' to make your point. It'll get the point across without being offensive. Frig is even in the Scrabble dictionary. This is one habit that's definitely worth changing.

Some good topics

By now, you're ready to figure out what topics are acceptable in the early conversations with a BB lady. The old adage is true about not speaking about religion or politics. Careers, travel, current events, are always good, but keep it light for the time being.

When engaging a BB lady in an early conversation, always start by asking a question. Always make her feel that her part of the conversation is as important as yours, or more so. Here are some good starter questions:

- What would you do if you won the Lotto?

Communication and Conversations

- What is unfinished on your bucket list?
- If you were to live your life over, what advice would you give yourself?
- In fantasy, what career would you have wanted?
- What are five of your all-time favorite songs?
- What are your five favorite singers/musicians?
- What are you good at doing? Not so good at doing?
- What are your five most favorite movies?
- When you were a child, what did you think you'd be doing as an adult?
- If you could have lunch with anybody in history, who would it be? In politics, entertainment, sports, religion, science, art, technology, medicine, etc.

These are all great group conversation topics. (For those who are curious, my personal answers are: Thomas Jefferson, Johnny Carson, Mickey Mantle, Mother Theresa, and Albert Einstein. My second choices would be: Teddy Roosevelt, George Carlin, Red Auerbach, Jesus, and Charles Darwin.)

If there is a lull in the conversation or just some uneasiness, try what I call the bi-gender name game. This is not to be confused with the 60's song..."The Name Game." Remember?

Shirley, Shirley, Bo-ber-ley, bo-na-na fanna, fo-fer-ley. Fee fi mo-mer-ley, Shirley!

BABY BOOMER WOMEN

When we were teenagers and that song would come on the radio, I would always come up with "Let's do Chuck!" I assume you get the picture... Me – always the class clown!

The bi-gender name game goes like this: simply pick out names that are used by both genders. It can be strictly by spelling (Pat, Dale, Robin). Another option is to do it by pronunciation (Francis/Frances, Lynn/Lynne, Terry/Teri), etc.

I know it sounds a little goofy, but it's just one more way to open the communication lines!

These are just suggestions, and everybody has their own style. Figure out your personal style! These are especially helpful for the shy guys.

In discussing careers and jobs, there is a good chance that she may have held more than one in her working career. Good starters are:

- What was your favorite job? Why?
- What was your least favorite job? Why?
- What were your most significant accomplishments in your career?
- What would have been your dream job that you never had?
- What advice did you give your children, or young people, about their careers?
- What education and training were necessary to perform well in your field?
- How has technology changed your career through the years?

If you enjoy travel and want to talk about her travel experiences, "What foreign countries have you visited?" sounds much better than, "I've been to such and such; what

Communication and Conversations

about you?" You may have visited the same places, so try to strike a common note about the food, people, or tourist sites and everyday life.

For example, let's say you have both been to Italy. Good conversation starters might be:
- When did you go?
- What cities did you see?
- Which city was your favorite?
- What sights did you see there?
- Did you like the food?
- Any favorite dishes that were unique to that area?
- Did you get a chance to see the countryside?
- Did you have any special or unusual circumstances on your trip?
- What were the best and the worst parts of your trip?

If you have both done some traveling around the USA, use that as a topic for some great conversations.
- Did you travel by car, RV, or whatever?
- Did you see any national parks?
- What was your favorite? Least favorite?
- Did you see any museums, historical sites, etc.?
- What cities did you enjoy?
- What states did you find most interesting?
- Where was the best food?
- Where were the friendliest people?
- What did you like the best?
- What do you still want to see?

It's great if you can add your two cents worth too, but let her speak. In a sense, this also gives her an opportunity to relive her good visit there.

Here's an idea that has worked well after some preliminary conversation. I preface this by saying that I am not a trained psychologist but I have been told that the symbolisms and representations are correct.

This is meant to be lighthearted, not some deep, dark inner soul searching. Ask her if she's willing to do some visualization. If she is, begin by explaining to her that she is out in the country or in the woods in a safe area. Tell her there is a path going through the woods and she has decided to take a walk on it. Keeping her in visualization, ask her the following questions:

Describe your path. Is it wide or narrow? Is it straight or curvy? Is it well beaten down or is it seldom used? Is it rocky and dangerous or is it smooth?

Walking further, she sees a key lying on the path. Describe the key. Is it new or old? Is it a small luggage key? Is it an old antique skeleton key? Is it a car key? What kind of key is it? Is it valuable? Does she pick it up?

Continuing on the path, she sees a cup. Is it a silver chalice? Is it a ceramic coffee cup? Is it a plastic or paper cup? What kind of cup is it? Is it valuable? Does she pick it up?

As she continues on the path, she encounters a body of water. Is it a lake, stream, ocean, puddle, or a river? Is it clean or polluted? Is it a picture postcard setting or is it set between some smokestack factories?

Have her imagine that she has now magically gotten to the other side of the water. She is still on the original path but now she encounters an obstruction across the path. Is it a ten-foot high brick wall? Is it a fence that can be climbed over easily? Is it a tree trunk that has fallen down? Is it a razor-edge barbed wire fence? Can she get around it with difficulty or is it easy?

She is now past the obstruction. What is after the obstruction? What does she now see? Does the same path continue for an unseen distance? Does it just end? Does it go to a pasture or clearing? Is there a house at the path's end? What does she see?

Now it's time for her to open her eyes. You now have a treasure trove of fascinating conversation waiting for the two of you! Remind her again that you are not a trained psychologist. This exercise is purely for fun. Explain to her that this is simply a snapshot of where she is today. Further explain that her visualization would be different if one of her loved ones had recently died or if she won the lottery recently.

Extreme sadness or happiness would also affect her visualization experience. By explaining that you are not a professional at this, it leaves the interpretation open to be discussed by both of you. In many cases, her answers will be close to her actual feelings and experiences. Sometimes, there may be disagreements, but in any case, you will have continued a conversation that can be fun and insightful.

Here's what the symbols mean

The PATH symbolizes her path in life. The width of the path indicates how many people she will have close to her as she goes through the path of life. If it's wide enough for only one, she may be a loner. If it's wide enough for two, she will probably want to travel on the path with a partner. If it's wide enough for a car or wider, she may want to have more people in her travelling group.

Was her path straight or twisted and curvy? If it's straight, she is headed in one direction without much variation. If it's curvy, she may be open to trying other things and may not have a specific goal in mind. If it's smooth, her visualization is for a smooth journey. If it's rocky and treacherous, she may see a rough, difficult journey ahead.

The KEY symbolizes education. This is pretty simple. Usually, but not always, the value of the key is in proportion to the educational level of the person. Don't misconstrue education with degrees. Education can be learned in numerous ways other than traditional school. For example, a person can have an MBA from a prestigious university but fail at running a business because they don't understand the concepts "courtesy" and "customer service." These are usually learned on-the-job by people who are street smart. As Tom Hopkins says, "There are two things necessary to be successful in business. People have to LIKE you and TRUST you."

I have enjoyed the privilege of being a guest lecturer to eighth semester, soon-to-graduate university seniors. Knowing these seniors were about to launch their careers, the title of my lecture was, "Think Like a Business Person; Think Out of the Box." I asked them to have a pencil and paper ready to answer two questions.

My first question was, "Not in arithmetic or mathematics, but in business, how much is one plus one?" After giving them a minute to write down their answers, I asked how many of them answered "two." Most of them did. I then explained that it wasn't a math or arithmetic answer I was looking for. I wanted a business answer. Although they were ready to receive degrees, they didn't yet understand business.

In business, one plus one equals three! You may have any of the following; just pick two of them. You may have capital, labor, ideas, patents, land, raw materials, infrastructure, and so forth. If you combine any two of them in business, you must create the third thing: PROFIT.

Profit is why entrepreneurs start businesses – to make money. You can have all the above named items, but when you put them together in business, you must make a profit. Thus, in business, one plus one equals three.

Now that they had the answer to question one, it was time for question two.

Question two: "Not in arithmetic or math, how much is two plus two?"

Most answered "five" or some other number but they all got it wrong. When I encouraged them to think outside the box, they still weren't thinking like a business person out of the box. Heck, everybody knows in basic arithmetic, two plus two equals four.

The correct answer in business to the question of how much is two plus two is: *"What figure did you have in mind?"*

This exercise was simply to show them that sometimes there is little correlation between being educated and being smart. My mentor, Bob Spink, had only one year of college but he was far and beyond the smartest person I have ever met. If you are smart, sometimes a formal education isn't needed, and if you have a formal education with a degree, don't fool yourself by thinking that you are therefore smart.

Back to our symbols.

The CUP symbolizes love. Granted there is very little chance of anyone finding a silver chalice in the middle of the woods, but this is our imagination, so just go with it. The point here is does she pick it up? If she picks it up, that indicates it has some value to her (even if she discards it later). If she steps on it before continuing down the path, it might indicate that she places little value in love. This may indicate a BB lady who has experienced bad relationships and messy divorces.

    The BODY OF WATER symbolizes sex. If she visualized a polluted pond or a dirty mud puddle, change the subject quickly. However, you will probably find that most BB women will see a postcard picture of a lake, river, or stream. This is a great time to act very learned and maybe add a little teasing about her answer. With regard to the size of the body of water, you might show some definite approval and interest. By no means should you make too much of a fuss about it; remember this is all just a way of getting to know each other.

    The OBSTRUCTION symbolizes death. This encompasses not only her own death, but also the death of her loved ones. This analogy is also pretty straightforward. If she finds it easy to get around the obstruction, then she understands that death is just part of our journey. I don't want to appear to be flippant about the subject but the fact remains we all die sooner or later. Some believe the death of a human body is simply a *transition* of the inner spirit to another dimension.

    A wise man once said, we're all on a death path from the moment we are born. For some the path is shorter than others. It's not exactly the way I want to look at life, but I do understand his reasoning. If she sees a huge insurmountable wall, she probably does not have the ability to come to terms with death. Obviously her answer would be impacted if she recently had a death in her circle of family and friends.

    AFTER THE OBSTRUCTION symbolizes our spiritual afterlife. This area is open to a lot of interpretation. For those who see a clearing, a pasture, or Grandma's house, they probably believe in the lessons from church about heaven and hell. Those who see the path just continuing, they may believe in reincarnation. For those who simply see the path ending, they might be atheists. In any scenario, be careful here as to not offend anyone's religious beliefs.

Bill was a friend of mine who was T-boned by a drunk driver in a horrific car crash. He was transported to a distant hospital in an enclosed ambulance. His mom and the driver were in the front and Bill and the paramedic were in the enclosed rear. At one point in the trip, Bill suddenly realized that he was riding above the ambulance. It was an amazing experience for him. As he later tried to describe it, he said it felt like the best "sex, drugs, and rock and roll" of his life, all combined in one.

As the ambulance made the trip to take Bill to the hospital, they passed another terrible car crash that had just occurred. There was no way to see this awful scene from inside the rear of the ambulance. There were no windows.

When they arrived at the hospital, suddenly Bill opened his eyes, startling the paramedic. You see, Bill had been clinically dead for over an hour! The next day as he was talking to his mom, he described in detail the accident scene his ambulance has driven past. His mom was able to verify the whole story, just as Bill "saw" it.

I am sure you have also heard stories of those who have come back from the dead. Some talk about shining bright lights or seeing a deceased relative. If you heard Bill tell his story, it would probably raise the hairs on your arm, just as it did mine.

Susan was a sweet lady who had fought a long valiant battle against cancer. Nearing the end, she was settled back in her

home, sleeping in a peaceful coma under the care of a hospice nurse.

Knowing the time was near, the living room was filled with the people Susan loved: her husband, teenage daughter, her mother, sister, and her best friend.

Finally the moment came. The hospice nurse walked into the living room and gently explained to the family that after about fifteen minutes of checking vital signs, she determined death had occurred. Susan had peacefully slipped away.

The family took about ten minutes to comfort each other and compose themselves before entering the bedroom for a final goodbye.

They encircled the bed, holding hands. After a few minutes, they prayed several tearful "Our Fathers" together, trying without success to hold back the flood of tears.

About thirty minutes after Susan's death, she suddenly, shockingly, raised her head slightly, groaned out the words "Our Father," before she fell back on the pillow and closed her eyes. In one last exhale, she released what looked like a cylindrical tube of steam two or three feet long. That "steam" floated up to a corner of the room, hovered for a few brief seconds, and then quickly dissipated.

It slowly dawned on this sweet circle of family and friends. They had been given the privilege of actually witnessing Susan's spirit leave her body!

Whew, heavy stuff!

Regardless of the topic, be attentive and LISTEN. Keep in mind that many BB women have a history of being married to a guy who rarely listened to her. Show her that you care

Communication and Conversations

about what she is saying. This ability will do wonders for a positive relationship with a BB lady!

Always remember the huge importance of the "C" for Communication.

7
The First Date: Do's and Don'ts

Before we can even start talking about that all-important first date, we need to talk about how to ask for it!

If you have already had a pleasant conversation with her, it might be a good time to ask for a date. Other times, it might be more prudent to ask for her phone number or email address.

There may be times when you can get neither. That doesn't mean you just quit! It means you rethink your strategy. Do you have a friend who could act as an intermediary? Ask him or her to ask for you. Always remember that everyone and every situation is different; some people are shy and others are more forward in their approach.

Sometimes you will have to be quick on your feet and try to adapt to whatever it is you think will work. Other times you may consider being a little more laid back. In any event, you will have to initiate the date request because most BB women will not do so.

Listen to what she says. She may drop a hint and if you're paying attention, you'll be ready. If you hear, "It'd be nice to see you again," follow up on that immediately. Having them actually ask you for a date will be rare.

Most importantly, DO NOT TRY SOME PICK-UP LINE! I cannot overstress this. BB women have heard it all. Just be yourself and show a sincere interest in meeting her.

As an exception to the above, I do have a suggestion that usually generates a laugh or a response. If you have hair, are bald, or even if you wear a rug, ask her this, "I have to ask you somewhat of a personal question. Is my toupee on straight?"

The First Date: Do's and Don'ts

If you are bald, it's a good chuckle. If you have hair, you may get a question in return. If you wear a toupee, it'll show that you're truthful! In any event, it can serve to break the ice.

Next, think about where you'll pick her up. With all the crazies in today's world, some BB women may be reluctant to have you pick her up for the first date at her home. This is understandable, so just go with it. If that is the case, just arrange to meet her wherever you are going. If the destination is out of town, meet her in some public parking lot (mall or supermarket) and car pool from there.

What NOT to do...

Sometimes it helps to know what NOT to do. Pay attention to these mistakes.

I have a relative who tells an almost unbelievable first date story. Sherry is retired, self-sufficient, and very attractive. She met Tom at a picnic. The two of them hit it off right away and she agreed to have a future dinner date with him.

On the day of their date, Tom arrived on time, dressed in business attire (with a tie and all). Sherry appreciated a well-dressed man. He explained that he had a hectic day at work and didn't have time to go home and freshen up before picking her up at her home. His next question shocked her.

Are you ready for this one?

"May I use YOUR toothbrush?" Not..."Do you have an unused spare?" Just, "May I use YOUR toothbrush?"

Yuck, Double Yuck, and Gag me with a spoon!

Although she did have a couple of new unused toothbrushes, she was so shocked by the question that she simply told him to leave.

BABY BOOMER WOMEN

Remember that hint about impeccable personal hygiene?

A dear friend Elaine tells another disaster first date story. Bob invited her to dinner and upon seating, he whipped out a newspaper that had the restaurant's ad for two-for-one specials. He proudly told her that she can feel free to order whatever she wants as long as it's on the two-for-one special list!

Elaine managed to hide her shock, but retaliated by ordering a bottle of expensive wine and a second desert to take home!

Smart Lady! I probably don't have to tell you this was their first ...and last date.

So, no matter your approach, let's assume she accepts. What now?

You may suggest something close to your heart, a sail in your boat, a flight in your plane, or a cruise on your motorcycle. If you have already made a connection with her on a specific topic, you might want to suggest that. If she likes art, suggest going to a museum or seeing an art show at a local college or gallery. If she's into sports, suggest a walk or bicycle ride.

For your first date, never suggest something competitive like tennis or golf. Swimming might not be a good idea either because some BB women may not want to be seen in a swimsuit on the first date. Whatever you suggest, listen to her suggestions too.

In fact, it is probably better to do something she suggests. There are two reasons for this. First, she will feel more comfortable in a situation that was her idea, and secondly (and possibly even more importantly), it shows you are willing to compromise. That will earn you brownie points throughout your possible upcoming relationship. Remember that getting a first date is nice, but showing her a good time on that first date will ensure more dates in the future.

Make sure she knows beforehand what you are going to do and where. This will give her an opportunity to be dressed properly for the date. Think it through! You may think you planned a great date and want to surprise her by going to a car race. But if she shows up wearing a dinner dress, how are you going to feel? Don't let that happen!

The goal for the first date is to get to know each other. You already started the process when you first met her. You had an initial conversation during that first meeting; now you want to establish a little more comfort level.

This is where two of the C's come into play: Chemistry and Compatibility. Never – repeat *never* – go to a movie on the first date! Why would you do that and then just sit for two hours without any conversation? How are you going to get to know someone without conversation? Additionally, she may be into chick flicks and you might like action movies. There will be plenty of time for movies in the future but not on the first date. This is very strict advice.

I know many men are shy, especially on first dates. Some women are too. If this is you, consider softening the situation by inviting a person or another couple with whom you are mutual friends. I do not recommend this unless shyness is an issue. It's just a way to relieve some potential uneasiness during conversation lulls or topic segues.

If you do this, be sure you invite someone who is pleasant but not overly talkative or overbearing either. This should be your time to chat with your date, not have to listen to a third party. You may also want to have a prearranged signal so the third party knows to make a graceful exit, leaving you alone with your date.

Sometimes including a third party is a great beginning but only if she agrees and only if they are the correct third party. Again, this is not always the best idea but you must be willing to do whatever it takes to get that first date and have it be a comfortable and enjoyable experience for both of you, but mostly for her.

Daytime or evening?

Do you invite her on a daytime date or an evening date? There are some factors to be considered here. What activity are you choosing? Where will you go? Do either of you have time constraints like having to wake up early for work or having to get home early to feed the dog? Is whatever you do or wherever you go more pleasurable or romantic during the daytime or the evening? Is a weekday better than a weekend date?

A visit to the local zoo is probably a better daytime activity since they are usually closed in the evenings. Would a midweek zoo trip be less crowded than on the weekends?

Dances, on the other hand, are usually held during the evenings.

A boat cruise could be either; it may be too hot during the afternoons and maybe a little more dangerous in the evening. It may be better to go during the week as the waterways are usually more crowded on weekends.

Whatever the activity or destination, some consideration must be given to the day and time for the first date.

Jason finally had a date with a gal he had worked on attracting for quite a while. She finally agreed. He was really

The First Date: Do's and Don'ts

looking forward to this first date and had planned on a leisurely dinner at a great restaurant.

But when the day came, winter weather did not cooperate. Travelling on the Interstate, Jason and his date were halfway across a bridge when he hit a patch of black ice. The car spun out of control several times before finally coming to a stop. Thankfully, his car ended up with just a very mild dent and there were no personal injuries.

Imagine being close to death twenty minutes into your first date with someone? The happy ending is that this great couple has now been married for over 40 years! It's a story they still love to tell.

Is a daytime lunch a better suggestion than an evening dinner? Either one could be great but it depends on the circumstances. A good rule of thumb is to do whatever she suggests or what she agrees to do in the event that you make the choice.

What are her food preferences? Is she a burger and fries gal, seafood lover, a vegetarian, vegan, or have some specific dietary restrictions? Are there some things she really enjoys for meals? Are there some things she refuses to eat? Some people are strict vegans. If so, where will you go?

Some people will eat poultry and fish but not red meat. Some folks will eat most everything except pork. If she is vegetarian and you are a meat lover, make sure the restaurant you choose offers soup and salad choices in addition to their regular meat dishes.

Here's something you may want to consider. If there is a huge disparity in your food preferences, how would it work out in the long run? Suppose she is vegan and you are a meat and potatoes guy. What would that really be like over time?

Or maybe she eats most everything but with a healthy slant to it. Would it work if your food choices are gobbling down bacon burgers, Buffalo wings, and greasy fries? This is the time to ask yourself if your food choices are compatible enough to work over the long haul. Make sure these questions are clarified before proceeding with dining choices. Did I say "Compatibility?"

Once a food type is selected, ask her if she has any favorite places that serve that type of food. Even if you are just going for an informal lunchtime pizza, ask for her suggestion.

My personal favorites are usually independent owner/operator or Mom & Pop restaurants. I prefer them to corporate owned chains because I like doing business with the owners. I enjoy thanking them for a nice meal instead of giving a dividend to the stockholders. There are however, many fine corporate owned chain restaurants.

This is the first date, so go along with wherever she wants to go. That way you will ensure she enjoys the location, the meal, and her time with you.

How to dress

This is your one and only chance to make a first impression! So be sure you are properly dressed for the occasion. Shorts or jeans are fine for a walk or an informal lunch but probably not acceptable for dinner in an upscale restaurant.

No matter the venue, do not wear a tee shirt for an evening date. A shirt with a collar is a requirement. I understand that there are BB women who are completely informal, but ZZ Top reminds us, "Every girl's crazy about a sharp dressed man!"

The First Date: Do's and Don'ts

I know a guy who was crazy about a BB woman and had tried to date her for some time. To his surprise, one day she invited him to her place for a light bite to eat and then a walk on the beach. He assumed that the walk on the beach meant an informal evening. Shorts, right? That was mistake #1.

Mistake #2? He assumed that driving over on his motorcycle would be perfect, thinking they might take an evening ride after the beach walk. Wrong!

Mistake #3: He got a late start. And because he was wearing a helmet on the ride over, he couldn't hear his cell phone ringing. She was calling to learn why he was late. By the time he got there, she was pretty upset.

So, he arrived late, dressed very casually in shorts, and walked up to her door to discover she has dressed up for the elegant, romantic dinner she had prepared. She looked classy and beautiful; he missed it by a mile.

It became apparent that she was absolutely turned off by his casual shorts. She had gone to a lot of trouble, and it made her feel disrespected.

He tried to save the day. He apologized profusely but in her eyes the night was already ruined. In fact, halfway through dinner, she asked him to leave.

Although it was all unintentional, he was heartbroken. The lesson to be learned is to be prompt and be appropriately dressed.

Sometimes it's a good idea to ask the lady what she is wearing or ask her what she would recommend for attire. When in doubt, you should over dress because you can always dress down. If you are under dressed, it's nearly impossible to dress upward.

At some point we have to resign ourselves to the fact that unless we change our eating and exercise habits, there will be some degree of unwanted belly in the mirror. Don't accentuate it by wearing tight clothing. Usually an over shirt or something worn over the belly (shirt tails out) tends to hide it somewhat. Vertical stripes are better than horizontal. Don't kid yourself by wearing a 36 inch belt with a 40-inch belly hanging over it!

And then, be punctual. Especially for that first date. Be on time. If you are just late for no excusable reason, you are in essence telling her she's not important enough to you to be on time. Shame on you if you're late! It will start the date off on a bad step.

Make it a point to be on time and show up with a sparkle in your eyes. Make her feel that you are excited about being with her and that you are grateful she accepted your invitation.

Flowers?

Yes, flowers! If you really are interested in this gal, bring her beautiful, fresh cut flowers. I know this may appear to be a little old-fashioned, but since manners and good grooming are also considered to be old-fashioned in today's world, just take my advice on this. You are reading this to hear my advice, now put some of it into practice.

However, don't overdo it. No big bouquet of roses! To bring a BB woman a dozen roses on the first date might scare her off. It's too much, too soon. Sometimes a single rose might work, but whatever it is, she will appreciate your thoughtfulness.

I recommend the Jay Ferry Bouquet. What the heck is that, you ask?

Go to the florist and order 6 - 8 stems of daises. Each stem has about 6 - 10 flowers and they come in white, yellow, pink, and even a shocking red. Ask the florist to put a single

The First Date: Do's and Don'ts

rose in the middle. Because roses come in so many colors, you can make a great color combination.

White daises look great with any color rose. Red daises look wonderful with a lighter colored rose. If you are unsure about the color combination, ask the florist for advice. They are professionals about floral arrangements so let them advise you. Make sure the flowers you get are fresh so they will last a little longer.

Then ask the florist to surround the daises with a few sprigs of baby's breath. Surround all that with some greens and have it all tied together with a wide ribbon, usually the color of the single rose. Have it wrapped in some florist paper and you're ready to go. This bouquet will last a lot longer and be less than half the price of a dozen plain old roses.

If you're a big jokester, wrap them in newspaper. She might get a laugh out of the contradiction between the mundane newspaper and the beauty of the bouquet.

This bouquet should cost about $20. Just to avoid a surprise, get a price from the florist before ordering.

What makes the Jay Ferry Bouquet significant? Well, she'll put it in a vase and off you go on your date. When she returns after the date, she'll have something nice to look at. If the date goes well, she'll appreciate your thoughtfulness. She'll know you treated her like a lady.

Over the next few days, every time she sees this bouquet, she'll think about you again. After five to seven days, the rose will die and she'll pull it out. When she discards it, who will she think of? You!

The daises will last a couple of weeks. During that time, some of the daises will wilt earlier than others. As she is trimming off the wilted ones, who will she think of? You!

When all the daises have died and she is throwing the last of them away, who will she think of? You!

We're not finished yet. Many BB women like to hang up the baby's breath to dry them for later use. Who does she think of when she's drying the baby's breath? You!

So the Jay Ferry Bouquet will keep you fresh in her mind for weeks after the first date. I am willing to bet that she will even compliment you again after the flowers are gone.

In the future as your relationship develops, flowers should become a regular part of your continuing admiration for her. Most BB men could care less about having fresh cut flowers around the house, so when you bring her flowers, they are primarily for HER.

If you go out to dinner, both of you get to enjoy a good meal. But flowers? That's just for her. They are an appreciative gift from you to her exclusively. You get nothing in return. It's just you letting her know how much she means to you.

Bring her flowers for no special reason. Bring them in the middle of the week. Bring flowers on significant dates. On the one-month anniversary of your first date. On her birthday. On Valentine's Day.

But under no circumstances, do you ever bring her flowers after an argument. You may end up wearing them as a suppository!

Minding your manners

Let's assume you haven't screwed up thus far. Because we're guys, we probably need a little review on basic manners. If you're one of the few who already has manners, congratulations.

The First Date: Do's and Don'ts

This is an area that cannot be taken lightly. If you don't have manners, you will not do well with a BB woman. This is an absolute requirement. I will lay this out in steps so you can use it like a pilot uses a checklist before takeoff. Memorize this and do not skip any steps.

Let's assume you are at her house and on the way to dinner.

- Ask her if she is ready to leave; do not assume it.
- Assist her in putting on her coat, jacket, etc.
- Open the door for her and allow her to pass through first.
- Open the car door and ensure that her legs and clothes are in before closing it.
- Once moving, drive as an adult, not a teenager.
- Ask her if the temperature is comfortable for her. Make adjustments as needed.
- If she wants music, ask her what she wants. If she has no preference, offer something smooth and easy. This is not the time for acid rock.
- If there is no music preference, keep the chatter light. A good topic is how much you're looking forward to a great meal with her.
- If the restaurant has valet parking, use it. If not, offer to drop her off at the door to wait for you while you park. If she wants to stay with you while you park, let her (that's a good sign).
- Open the door to the restaurant and allow her to enter first.
- Remove your hat immediately. Nothing shows a complete lack of manners and upbringing more

than a grown man wearing a hat or a ball cap in a restaurant.
- Ask her if she has a preference in seating and relay her suggestion to the host/hostess.
- Ask her if the table selection is to her liking before being seated.
- Pull out her chair and assist her in pushing it back in.
- If she has a drink, have one yourself. Do not ever drink more than she does.
- When the menus arrive, show courtesy and respect for the server.
- Ask if there are any chef's specials in addition to the menu items.
- Discuss her and your favorite items on the menu.
- Order for her. Never say, "She'll have." It's always, "The lady would like to order the such-and-such." Make sure you know how it is prepared and that she likes the food prepared and seasoned that way.
- Use proper table manners. In the event that you are a little unsure of what is proper, find out before your date! There are many articles written about table manners. Generally speaking, use the silverware from the outside of the plate going inward to your plate. Also make sure that the napkin is in your lap, not on the table or used as a bib.
- Never order soup on the first date. It could be messy or noisy.

The First Date: Do's and Don'ts

- Make sure you continue the conversation during dinner. If you run out of topics, you can always discuss the food or the restaurant décor, etc.
- When the server returns to check on you, even if you already know the answer, ask her if everything suits her properly. She may want another napkin or something else, so ask.
- When the meal is finished, ask her if she would enjoy dessert. If not, ask her if she might like to split one of her choice.
- When settling the bill, make sure you compliment the server and the food. Even if it is just average, a compliment will show her that you are enjoying her company regardless of the food and service.
- Tip generously, (at least 20%). Figure the tip in your head. For you math-challenged guys, multiply the total by two and move the decimal point one digit to the left. Do NOT ever be a cheap tipper. This is a major embarrassment to both you and her.
- Reverse the order when leaving. Help her with her chair, coat, door, etc.
- Tip the valet generously.

I know of a guy who was an ex-military officer. However, his upbringing completely lacked any kind of class. As an adult, he actually ate caveman style with his utensils, slurped his soup, drinks, and food. He chewed his food with his mouth open, making disgusting noises while he was eating. Before the server could remove the dishes, he would pile them up as one would do in a cafeteria.

Once, at a very swanky, private supper club the waiter was serving the aperitif between courses and this guy remarked, "What a great place this is. They bring the sherbet even before dessert, but mine isn't very lemony tasting." Imagine the horrified embarrassment of the host, not to mention the good laugh the staff had back in the kitchen!

I knew of another classless guy who was on a first date that included her adult children. Pushing his chair from the table, he announced, "I'm gonna take a leak." He left without noticing the stunned look on everyone's faces. The adult children just stared at their mother in shocked silence. Did he really just say that? The mom knew exactly what their expressions meant. *What kind of a person are you bringing into our family?*

When she confronted him later he sarcastically responded, "Okay, next time I'll say it like my father used to say, "I've gotta go see a man about a horse."

Remember what I said in the beginning about communication?

So take this time to brush up on your manners, but keep in mind, there may be some women still holding on to the Women's Lib days of unshaven legs and bra burning. If she says she can open her own doors, you should still try to do so unless you discover that she actually means it. If so, apologetically say that you were raised with manners and you were simply trying to show her the respect she deserves. Gently state that you try to show respect to all people by having manners, not only for a date, but for everyone.

Personally, when I enter a building, I still hold the door open for either gender.

The First Date: Do's and Don'ts

After dinner

Once you have left the restaurant, ask her if there's somewhere else where she would like to go. There may be a cocktail lounge, dance, or something else to do to extend the evening. This will also give you a good indication of how she is mentally rating your evening to this point. If she suggests something, just go with it. Remember the drill, start by opening her door and doing the other things previously discussed.

There are many intangible mistakes that can be made out of sheer selfishness and stupidity. Learn a lesson from Ted.

Carol and Bob and Ted and Alice were on a double date for dinner. Carol and Bob were a long term couple, but Ted and Alice had dated only a couple of times. After an enjoyable evening, they were headed home. Bob was driving with Carol in front beside him; Ted and Alice were in the back seat. The four were chatting about the meal and the restaurant.

Gradually, Bob realized that Ted had stopped participating in the conversation. A glance into the rear view mirror told the whole story. Ted was playing solitaire on his phone! Bob looked at Carol and they exchanged knowing glances. She had seen it too. The stupid game and phone were more important to Ted than being present in a friendly conversation. How insulting to his date! How crass and ignorant! Although Alice had been warned by her gal pals, she has continued to date the schmuck!

Her horniness will keep a relationship going for a while, but it simply won't last long. She is a classy lady and he is a self-absorbed moron. I do not believe that opposites attract. But sometimes, with extenuating circumstances, they do. At least for a while.

The lesson here is: don't let the phone run your life!

At the end of the evening, you will return her to the place where you picked her up for the date. Walk her to her car or house. This is a great time to let her know again that you enjoyed the evening. Once at the door, read her body language to determine what to do next. Some of her signals will be obvious and you can go with it.

If you are unsure, use caution and go slowly. If you're not getting any positive feedback, just attempt a warm hug and maybe a soft peck on her hair or forehead.

No handshake here; you're trying to start a friendship, not trying to be her minister. Let her know that you'd like to see her again and set a date if she's willing. If the response seems lukewarm, don't push it.

Let her know that you appreciate the date and the opportunity to get to know her a little. Compliment her again on something – her attire, choice of restaurant, her smile, or whatever made the deepest impression on you. A ton of sincerity is needed here. Sincerely ask her if it would be okay to contact her again. If so, when? Ask if she prefers a call, email, or text?

This would also be a good time to set a venue for the next date. She may like to go for a walk, see a concert, a sporting event, enjoy a home cooked dinner prepared by either of you (see my easy recipe ideas in the Appendix), or whatever else she may want to do. If she has no preference, suggest a couple of things. Just let her make the final decision, not you.

If she does not readily accept, don't be pushy. Let it simmer for a bit of time. It may take her a little while to reflect on the first date before making a decision to go on another. She may want to talk to her girlfriends first.

If you never hear from her again, don't be discouraged. It may or may not be you. She may have other interests in mind. Enjoy the fact that you were gracious and had a nice time. Remember: Chemistry!

For whatever reason, she may not be attracted to you, but she may know of somebody who could be. I knew a guy who met several women on the internet. When he first met face-to-face, if he knew he wasn't interested in her, he would ask if she had any unusual experiences from computer dating. That would be his main topic of conversation. Later, when it was time to leave, he would ask if she knew anybody she thought might be interested in having a date with him. It may sound ridiculous, but it actually does work.

So, assuming she agrees to continue with you, be sure you communicate using the medium she prefers. Did she say she wants a phone call, text, or email? Some BB women like to chat, others to text, email, or whatever.

If you are on Facebook or other social media sites, be especially careful of what you post. Don't make too much or too little of your date. It's probably best to not post anything at all this early in your relationship.

If you sometimes find it difficult to find the right words to express your feelings, find a song that fits what you want to say. If you're a decent singer and brave, sing it to her! Otherwise, write out the words and send it or say it to her.

There's a song for every feeling and situation known to mankind. Again, sincerity and truthfulness are paramount. (Incidentally, never use the lyrics of any song without saying which song it came from. You could look pretty bad being caught plagiarizing song lyrics while trying to pass them off as a self-written poem!)

Everybody is in your life for a reason.

BABY BOOMER WOMEN

By now you should start to get the picture. Be accommodating, flexible, and fun to be with. Being a pushy, rigid sourpuss will get you nowhere.

8
Moving Forward

You may have now had several "first dates" and maybe they haven't worked out successfully. This is just the way life is. There may be some really fine BB women who, for whatever reason, just didn't click with you and vice versa.

By now, you can tell my admiration for BB women is obvious. However, with just the law of averages, there will be some BB women you should just stay away from. There are *users* who appear to be *friends.* They name streets after people like that...ONE WAY! Users can use your money, time, friendship, emotions, hospitality, and anything else. What do they give back? Only a little. Look for the imbalance. It should be give-and-take. Both partners should give. Both partners should take. It's all about balance.

And then there are some who are looking for Mr. Sugar Daddy. You may not figure this out at first. Some have the ability to make it appear that money isn't their prime motivation. Give it time. It will become obvious with time.

Remember: we all have histories and in some cases they haven't been pretty. It could take years to recover from an abusive relationship. There are some who may never recover. I call them "Damaged Goods." This can be someone of either gender but generally it means someone is unwilling or unworthy to start a relationship.

This is okay. Remember: Compatibility, Communication, and Chemistry. Just remember that these women are still good networking possibilities. If someone liked you, she may actually recommend you to a friend, or a friend to you. Either way, unless your date was an absolute disaster, it's wise to stay on good terms with her. Actually, it's a good idea to be on good terms with everyone. The universe will accept your good energy and send it back to you.

For now, let's assume you have gotten a second or third date. Don't try to hit a home run. Even a bunt single gets you on base. Building a relationship takes time; don't try to rush it.

If you are serious about improving your life by limiting your network TV intake, try some of the old fashioned stuff like cards and board games. Cribbage, rummy, and pinochle are excellent two-handed card games. Chess, Monopoly, and Scrabble are great board games. Play Scrabble with a Scrabble Dictionary…Wow!

Card games and board games allow a glimpse of someone's thought processes and their competiveness. And it's a fun way to spend an evening!

Speaking about loyalty does not prove anything. Loyalty can only be proven over time. It's a virtue that is paramount to BB women. Many of them have had past relationships where loyalty has been destroyed. If that has happened to her, it's going to take time for you to earn her trust.

Remember: Commitment.

I know of a guy who met a wonderful lady on the internet and after one date announced that "this is the woman I will spend the rest of my life with."

Oddly enough, he had said that on several previous occasions because his shallowness is mostly based on his estimate of when he'll get her into bed. Although he thinks he is being loyal to her, he continued his bizarre fantasy by communicating online with Nigerian prostitutes.

His description of his lady is as he once said about her, "the men like to dance with her because she puts out." How crude, disrespectful, and disloyal can he be?

Moving Forward

If you want to continue building a quality relationship with a BB lady, loyalty must be included as the reinforcing iron bar in the cement of the foundation. If you are not willing to make that commitment, do not fool yourself into thinking that you can proceed. It will not work.

If you're shallow, admit it. You're a grown man. You can continue having shallow relationships if that's what you want. I guess that works for some BB men (and some women too). For some people, being in a committed relationship is not what they want. If that's you, be honest about that early in your communication so you don't lead her on or waste her time if she is looking for commitment.

I know of a couple who had dated for over ten years. She wanted children but he always came up with some excuse to not have one right now. He put her off for so long that her biological clock expired and they broke up. Although she is generally a happy, vivacious lady, she despises him to this day.

Imagine what a BB lady would think if you announce to the world that you are loyal. She'd be questioning why anybody would come out with such a stupid statement. Trumpeting this announcement sounds suspiciously hollow.

Loyalty isn't something to be announced! It's something you live. It's who you are. It's what you do day-in and day-out.

However, there are a few ways you can begin to display your loyalty. The first is to be clear with her about the past women in your life. You must make it crystal clear that whatever past relationships you may have had are now completely over.

There are very few exceptions to this rule. One may be financial commitments (alimony, child support, loans, etc.) that must be recognized. There may even be ongoing friendships with past lady friends. This will be okay as long as you clearly spell out the basis for those friendships and how it all works.

Darlene was a BB woman who had a four year relationship with Tim. Tim was basically a good guy; however, he blew the chance of being with Darlene forever. They mutually agreed to move on, but they did remain friends.

Eventually, she moved on and met Darrell. When Darrell questioned the status with Tim, Darlene explained their history. In addition, she offered to cut off all communication with Tim if that's what Darrell wanted. This confirmed her loyalty to him and in the end, the three of them got along well. They even played cribbage and pinochle together and dined together occasionally. Trust is huge.

You must convince her that whatever happened in the past is now completely over.

We have all heard the phrase, "When one door closes, another one opens." Reverend Dr. Joe Hooper of the Center for Spiritual Living in Palm Desert, California has a unique perspective on this. He says, "When one door closes, lock it up and seal the door, never to be opened again!"

This will keep you from wasting time thinking about why it happened or even dreaming that it might change. Close that door, lock it, and nail it shut. Never leave her guessing about past relationships. The only way you will convince her of your loyalty is to be absolutely honest about it.

There will be times when you will be discussing events in your past that includes past partners. Here you must not only be completely truthful, but don't dwell or expand on them too much. It's fine to discuss a wonderful vacation, but there is no need to expand on the details about the past lady.

For example, if it was a great vacation spot, tell her that you would like to share that experience with her too. Be careful here because it could backfire on you! Just go with your BB lady's wants and decisions. Don't mistake this for being an overly pleasing wimp; make the decisions based on the compromise of mutual likes.

Compatibility, yes?

Find ways to reassure her. Tell her she has the attributes that please you so much you would never consider wandering away from her.

Michelle was a widow who eventually had a fiancé who passed away while they were engaged. She felt that she would never again find "Mr. Right" ...until she met Jim.

Jim was a gentleman. Successful, kind, generous, and handsome. She thought the world of him. On their first weekend get-away, they chose a swanky resort. Michelle was really looking forward to a relaxing, enjoyable weekend together with this kind man she was coming to adore.

When they arrived, Jim opened his trunk and proudly showed off his golf clubs. Michelle managed to hide her shock. Surely he wasn't planning to use them here! Not on "their" weekend together! Wasn't it clear? This was their weekend to spend time *together!*

It soon became apparent that Jim absolutely had plans for those clubs. Michelle's expectations were headed for a huge crash. Jim told her (he didn't ask; he *told* her) he definitely planned on a round of golf. In fact, he cheerily wished her well as he headed out almost as soon as they checked in.

Michelle sighed. Okay, maybe he just needs a round of golf. It was a beautiful championship course.

As it turned out, Jim not only played 18 holes, but then went on to play the back nine *a second time.* When he finally returned, he was exhausted. After a quick shower, he turned on the TV to watch the golf channel. He basically ignored Michelle.

Dinner should have been time to reconnect, but that didn't happen either. Jim rushed through dinner. Why? Because he wanted to get back in time to catch the last few holes of a major tournament. Obviously, Michelle was not a priority to him.

Michelle took it all in. Glad when the weekend was finally over; she promptly dumped him.

Smart Lady!

Denise thought she had met the most wonderful man. Greg had all the qualities she thought she wanted in a man.

On their first weekend sleepover at his house, Greg spent the entire day tinkering with his classic Corvette. Thinking they would connect over dinner and through the evening, Denise was again disappointed. He spent the evening watching TV car programs. Denise quickly learned that the Corvette was more important to him than she was.

It didn't take long for her to make a decision. Planning a breakup was clearly the next thing.

Sometimes life brings surprises, and before she could dump him, he became quite ill. Feeling sorry for him, Denise decided to stick it out, at least until he regained his health.

When he recuperated, guess what? The Corvette took precedence again. Because of her unwarranted loyalty, she wasted a whole year of her life. Fortunately, she did move on.

Greg? He is still alone… and in love with a stupid car.

Moving Forward

Men just naturally look at women. I have seen it all the way from my two-year-old grandson to my ninety-year-old mentor. Within reason, this is okay because, in case you've been under a rock, you already know women look at men too! However, it must be within limits.

I once heard a lady tell her guy, "You don't look at women; you devour them!" This is not acceptable. Never let your lady feel that you would be tempted to stray because you're so busy admiring another woman's beauty or body. How would you feel if you knew she was wishing you had a flat tummy, big biceps, or a full head of hair while you catch her subtly admiring other men?

Granted there are some things that can be modified or even surgically reduced or enhanced. If those things are that important to you, then put it into perspective. A washboard tummy can be achieved, but being three inches taller cannot. If, in your mind, the physical appearance of another woman is really more important to you than your lady's current looks, then that's real trouble.

Rick was in a department store with his wife, Colleen. Colleen was a few feet away from Rick, looking at items a few feet away. She was a very cute pixie type although she had ridiculously large breast implants (because that's what her previous husband wanted). Two other men were standing near Rick, bored because their own matronly looking wives were shopping a few feet away. The other two men did not know that Rick was married to the cute Colleen.

They made crude comments about Colleen's chest and described the sexual things they would do to her if they had the chance. Their boastful conversation was demeaning, vile, and perverted.

BABY BOOMER WOMEN

Rick said nothing. He just waited until the other two wives returned and were within earshot. He then repeated exactly the perverted conversation he'd just heard from the other two men about his wife. Seeing the shocked faces was enough. Rick turned and walked away to join his wife.

It would have been fun to be a fly on the wall when those two matronly women got those husbands back home!

I know of another guy who watches a lot of TV. Whenever he sees almost any woman on the screen, he announces, "I'd **** that." Not even a "her", but a "that." Imagine how his lady – or any lady – would feel?

By now, you should get the picture that many BB women have had trials and tribulations and are very aware of what they want and how they want to be treated.

Always make her know she is #1. There is no #2.

Do the little romantic things often.

Remember the Jay Ferry Bouquet!

Say what's in your heart and more importantly, show it in your actions as much and as often as you can.

This "C" stands for Commitment.

9
Keep it Rolling?

After a few dates, things should be starting to gel. You should be feeling more comfortable with each other and the walls of privacy should be starting to crumble little by little.

If that is not the case, it might be time for a frank discussion about where you are heading as a couple. Some people need more time to analyze a potential decision than others and that's fine, but after a few dates both parties should know if they are willing to proceed.

If not, then not.

There may be some disappointment on either side, but the fact is that sometimes you just don't click no matter how much you may have wanted it. Everybody is in your life for a reason. Don't fret about something that didn't work; take whatever was positive about the experience and move on.

Meeting the family and the girlfriends

One of the upcoming hurdles for you to overcome will be to meet her children, grandchildren, and friends.

You must understand that passing the girlfriend test is critical. If her girlfriends don't like you, she will hear about your weak or negative points whenever they have their girl time together. If they do like you, they will be your best allies and supporters. The same is true for her couple friends as some of these people will become part of your social circle.

It's basically no different than what your friends will think about her. Hopefully, your true friends will give you an honest opinion of her and what they think your chances are of making it as a couple.

Their opinions are important but they are by no means the final word. Listen to them, but don't let their opinions overrule what you are thinking and feeling. Try to visualize what the future social circumstances might be like. Do this by mixing her with your friends as well as you mixing with her friends. Hopefully, the expansions of friendships will blossom on both sides.

Meeting the families, children, and grandchildren is far more important. Don't mess this up. Take care to make a strong positive impression with each one of them.

Chris met what he thought was the world's most wonderful woman. He and Sally had a short, torrid romance, quick engagement, and were soon married, although it met with considerable disapproval from his friends.

After moving in to his home, jealously showed its ugly face. Sally demanded that he only dance with women she first approved.

Her demands only got worse. When his children came to visit him in his own home, Sally gave them a thirty minute time limit per visit. Even worse, if he visited his children at their home, Sally would sit in the car and honk the horn after half an hour. Fortunately for him, he was smart enough to divorce her quickly!

I know of a BB woman whose mom tells her not to bring any man to meet her until she has dated him for at least a month. Actually, that makes pretty good sense. As she puts it, "You meet a lot of frogs before you meet the prince!"

Take enough time to be sure there is some possibility that your budding romance will bloom before involving either her family or your family. Never lose sight of the fact that she has

Keep It Rolling?

had a previous husband(s) and boyfriend(s). Why? Because you are going to be compared to them. No way around it. Accept it and just be ready.

You will be under scrutiny. Comparisons will be made. This is especially true with grandchildren. As grandparents we set the example. Don't confuse children by intermingling short term passion with the real deal.

With her children, there are several factors to be considered. How long has she been single? Was she divorced or widowed? Did she share a happy or unhappy relationship with her ex? What was the kids' relationship with the former husband or partner?

You may have huge shoes to fill or you might look like the knight in shining armor. Regardless, you must know the good or bad relationships of all parties concerned.

There is a huge difference between a relationship and an arrangement. Was she with a man where they shared a true love and respect for one another? Or was she in a loveless arrangement (or even a marriage) where they stayed together for the children, status, money, or some other silly reason?

You may discover that many BB women thought they were in a relationship, but eventually learned they were merely in an arrangement. Granted, love does change somewhat over time, but a continued relationship is based on love whereas an arrangement is based on other minor things.

It's very important to discover the status of her past relationships before you meet her family. Was he the right type of man for her? What were his strengths and weaknesses?

In any case, you are you; just be aware of her past. Don't try to change yourself to fit the mold of the previous guy. It's great and sometimes necessary to adapt and modify, but don't change. You are who you are and drastic change will probably be short lived and not sustainable over the long haul.

As one great Naval philosopher says, "I am what I am and that's all what I am" (Popeye, the Sailor Man).

The qualities I have previously discussed are equally if not more important when meeting the family.

- Grooming/Hygiene
- Manners
- Loyalty
- Integrity

Try to think of meeting women as if you were going on a job interview or a tryout for whatever. You must impress them in a positive way, yet be yourself at the same time.

All people and situations are different. Sooner or later, intimacy becomes part of the relationship. It may happen early, after meeting the family, or anywhere in between, but it will occur.

One BB woman told me she won't even kiss on the first three dates. Others feel comfortable with intimacy by the fourth date. Incidentally, the fourth date is the national average for intimacy. This is skewed because that includes all ages and I suspect it might be different in the BB generation.

Just remember you are no longer dealing with youthful inexperience. I have heard so many BB women tell me the biggest mistake many BB men is to rush into intimacy too early for their comfort.

So be patient. Remember that BB women have a past life – some good and others not so good. They are not concerned

Keep It Rolling?

with pregnancy, so many of them are more relaxed than they were in their younger years.

Some have a stronger passion drive than others so don't shift into overdrive while she is still in first gear. I have found that concerning intimacy, it's best to tell her you are on her timetable. This is an excellent way to put her at ease while also showing her that you genuinely care about her and the prospects for long-term commitment.

For most BB women, sex is not a frivolous act. Bluntly stated, they want to be loved, not screwed. Take the time to let things evolve and they will happen naturally. I know a BB guy who stayed overnight and slept – actually *slept* – with his BB lady about a dozen times before they enjoyed the Big Whoopee.

I know of another BB man who actually pulled the following antic. He had been with a BB woman for several dates and wanted to proceed to intimacy. She did too but was a little hesitant. He asked to stay over at her place and she softly declined.

He then said, "Okay, I'll see you in the morning." She agreed and asked what time. He replied, "When you get up, because I'll be sleeping in my car in your driveway." His playfulness was what she needed to hear. She relented and it was a win-win for both of them without any undue pressure.

You may find that intimacy after 60 is more rewarding and greater results are achieved.

Just some off-the-cuff experiences in this regard. Many BB women feel more comfortable in their own home when leading up to intimacy. Generally this is true if they live alone.

It certainly will not be true if she has kids, a roommate, or parents living with her.

But generally, in her own home, she is completely familiar with her surroundings, feels safe, and has all of her personal items already there (toothbrush, bath robe, hair products, etc.). Incidentally, all single BB men should keep an unused toothbrush and clean underwear somewhere in his car. One never knows when they might be needed.

Develop your own intimacy vocabulary with her. Avoid crass terms for her body parts. Many BB women like to refer to their breasts as Their Girls. Some like to call their panty area, as Barry White would say, their Secret Garden. A cute term for their backside might be their Tush.

She may suggest a playful name for your manhood. In any case, you both decide on the names for those areas and keep it light and happy. Always ensure that she knows that it's her you love and not just the body parts.

By now, BBs of both genders may have some surgical scars or other things that we didn't have in our 20s. Always remember that neither of you are unblemished anymore. Be sure to love the person, not just the body.

Those three words

For some BB men, there is some lingering fear of saying those three words, "I Love You." Some feel that the other person must say it first. Obviously there is no love in the first few dates. There may be great infatuation or strong attraction, but don't confuse that with love.

Tom boasts that in the first ninety minutes with a date, he can tell if he will spend the rest of his life with her. *You must be joking!*

In many languages there are several words that mean love. There are different kinds of love. Love for a parent is different than love for a child, which is different than love for a

Keep It Rolling?

pet, which is far different than the love of a food or a sports team or entertainer.

Love at our age is not shallow nor is it frivolous. By now, it's the real thing or nothing. If you feel it and you're ready to say the words out loud, don't just blurt it out. Have some conversation about how you both feel.

You might try a "temporary" love. I love you this weekend or on this cruise, but Monday we'll get back to normal on trying to build our relationship that will lead to a more permanent love.

You might have some special song whose lyrics more closely define your feelings. There's a wonderful song titled "831"...eight letters, three words, one feeling! Nice thought and a lovely way to express it.

A more laid back way to approach it could be to say, "Tell me when it's the right time to tell you." If she asks what you mean, just answer, "You know." I guarantee she will know and she will ask you to tell her when she wants to hear those words from you.

Just one more thought on this topic: If you don't truly feel it deep in your heart, don't say it.

10
And Away We Go...

I assume that all BBs will remember those words from The Greatest – Jackie Gleason. "And away we go..."

Gleason was known as "The Greatest" long before Muhammad Ali self-proclaimed that he was The Greatest. Granted, Ali was the greatest boxer, but I remember him mostly as America's Greatest Draft Dodger. In Vietnam, there were 58,600 lives sacrificed, tens of thousands of them African-Americans, while Ali stayed home pretending to be a clergyman.

"And away we go" means this reading is drawing to a close. I hope it helps you find that special person for the final lap around the track before your physical time on this earth comes to a close.

Think of your life as a four-lap race around a track. Each lap lasts about twenty years or so.

- In the first lap, you are just finding out about the track and learning about yourself and your abilities.

- In the second lap you are trying to get ahead at full speed, going as fast as you can, sometimes resulting in a few crashes.

- By the third lap you've learned when it's time to put the pedal to the metal and how to negotiate safely around the curves. In the first three laps the goal is to win, win, win.

- In the fourth and final lap, you are in cruise control, at a steady speed, waving to the crowd as you pass by. The objective has changed.

You're not as focused on winning. You're comfortable looking at simply finishing safely. You're glad to have your friends and family joyously joining you at the finish line.

This may be too simple of an analogy for some, but it reflects my experience while on this planet.

We are now in the final lap and lucky to be here. For a variety of reasons, many BBs did not get this far. If this book has somehow helped you to allow the cosmic energy to allow you to successfully cross paths with your soul mate, I will have achieved my goal in writing it.

Advice for both genders: Be aware when it comes to trying to get with a person who has recently had a relationship fizzle. It may take some time to heal emotionally. Some people may just not be ready to explore the possibilities of being with a new person in their lives. The previous partner may have been the world's best or an absolute jerk. You may have big shoes to fill or you may become the new Prince Charming. In either scenario, be patient, go slow, and give them abundant time and space to heal. It will give the new relationship a much better chance of success.

My final advice

- Chemistry
- Communication
- Compatibility
- Commitment

Let her know every day how much she means to you. How? Simply by being polite and courteous.

BABY BOOMER WOMEN

Saying "I Love You" is great but sometimes it sounds like rote recitation. Phrase it differently; it'll sound brand new.

Listen to her. Make sure she knows that what she says is important to you. Always do more than that. Give her feedback and comments on what she is saying. When you do, she will respond in kind.

Give her lots of hugs, not the sisterly ones, but the ones filled with tenderness, compassion, and caring. It's also nice to throw in a tush squeeze now and then to remind her of how attractive she is to you. Cuddling produces lots of warm fuzzies.

Give her flowers for no reason at no particular time. Every once in a while, pick some wildflowers for her.

Women appreciate being appreciated. Always treat your lady with love, kindness, and respect. I have known several men who are indifferent to their lady's wishes but then expect her to be ready to hop in the sack whenever he's in the mood. And then he doesn't understand why she isn't erotically responsive. This, my friend, is NOT how it works. In a sense, foreplay should be ongoing throughout each day. How? By showing her you love, respect, and care for her. The guy who said "Happy Wife, Happy Life" was spot-on correct!

Do things together, especially volunteering to help those in need: veterans, handicapped, elderly, homeless, and others. It will keep you centered and make you more grateful and appreciative of what you share together.

Occasionally send a card or a handwritten note. Make an attempt at writing a poem or use the lyrics from a meaningful song.

Make her smile. Make her laugh.

Always make things right by the end of the day. Never end the day with an argument.

And Away We Go...

Be positive, don't complain. Find a positive solution to any issue.

Most importantly, have trust in yourself that she is the right person for you. When you think that way, it will show in all aspects of your life.

There have been some memorable lines from movies. "Go ahead, make my day," or "We need a bigger boat." I have a couple of my own.

"My friends have overlooked my shortcomings, brought me through my dark days, and brightened the rest of them."

After everything was lost and there was no hope, Zorba was asked, "What do we do now?"

He simply replied, "Let's Dance!"

And so it is...

Appendix I
Great Easy Recipes

There are some BB men who think they have two left thumbs. They feel out of place in the kitchen.

This is not true and if you are willing, every man can learn to prepare a few easy dishes. This kitchen avoidance may be partially because you had a mom, wife, or girlfriends who were excellent cooks... or horrible cooks!

Or maybe some men were simply too lazy or felt that frozen dinners and canned vegetables were enough.

Wrong! Those foods are loaded with chemical preservatives, many of which are very harmful to your good health.

If you really have no confidence in your cooking ability, attend a basic cooking class. I assure you that there will be BB women attending. Who knows what could develop from that? Networking is always a good way to meet new people and possibly a quality BB woman.

Me? I am by no means a chef. All these recipes have been handed down by my mom, wife, or friends. Try preparing them with a BB woman to prove to her that you are not a clod in the kitchen. Cooking is a great way to spend quality time together.

Here are a few of my favorite quick and easy recipes. All of this works for a new or ongoing romance. It's also a perfect place to steal a smooch or two and sneak in a hug now and then.

Afterward, it is a perfect time to enjoy a private (candlelit?) dinner or a great evening with friends. When dinner is finished, make sure you initiate the cleanup. Do not expect to work in the kitchen and then have her clean up the mess you made! This is a critical mistake!

Being a partner in the kitchen produces more than great meals! It adds joy to an every day event!

If she likes chocolate...Chocoholic Pudding is the right choice.

When the early explorers of the new world eventually brought nuns with them, the natives taught the nuns about this wonderful new ingredient. They called it cocoa. The nuns learned to use it in baking and other dishes.

However there was soon a problem. None of the chocolate made its way back to the King in Spain. Why? The nuns ate it all!

Most women like chocolate; some seem to be addicted to it. If you really want to impress her and win the approval of her friends, prepare this dessert but ask her to wait to taste it. Give it to her when she is going to spend some time with her girlfriends. You'll be a hit with her and the Gal Pal Jury. Her girlfriends will like you even before they meet you. Trust me on this one.

Chocoholic Pudding

Mix 1/2 stick softened butter and 8 oz. cream cheese, then add 1 large container of chocolate (or regular) whipped topping (thawed), 2 small boxes instant chocolate pudding, 1 cup sugar, 1 cup chocolate milk, (squirt in a bunch of chocolate syrup for good measure).

Mix thoroughly. Use an 8x10 pan. Remove center filling from a bag of Oreos, (or your favorite chocolate cookie, but not chocolate chip). Crush half of the Oreos to line pan bottom, then add the above mixture. Top with remaining crushed Oreos.

OPTIONAL: You can top it all with shredded dark, white, or milk chocolate. Or arrange Hershey's kisses in the shape of a heart! Chill in fridge.

Buffalo Chicken & Potato Casserole

1 3/4 lbs skinless chicken breast
1/2 cup buffalo wing sauce
3 slices cooked chopped bacon
1 cup shredded Mexican blend cheese
24-28 oz bag gold potatoes
1 cup French fried onions
1/2 cup cut scallions
1/2 cup ranch dressing

Cut potatoes into half or thirds and microwave on high for 8 minutes. Drain them and toss with ¼ cup of buffalo sauce and transfer to 9 x 13 baking dish. Bake for 20-25 minutes @ 450 degrees. Stir once halfway through.

Cut cooked chicken into ½ inch cubes, toss with ¼ cup wing sauce, stir into potatoes. Combine remaining ingredients, top chicken and potatoes.

Bake 15-18 minutes. Center of casserole should be 165 degrees. Remove from oven, let stand 5 minutes and serve.

Slow Cooker Spaghetti Sauce

Cook 1 lb. lean ground beef and 1 lb. Italian sausage till no longer pink. Drain and transfer to 5 quart slow cooker.

Add:
1 medium chopped pepper (red or yellow)
1 chopped medium onion
8 cloves minced garlic
3 cans (14.5 oz.) Italian diced tomatoes drained
2 cans (15 oz) tomato sauce
2 cans (6 oz) tomato paste
1/3 cup sugar
2 Tb. Italian seasoning
1 Tb. basil
1 tsp. dried oregano
1 tsp. salt
1/2 tsp. pepper

Cook on LOW for 8 hours. Serve over your choice of pasta. Try it over Bucatini. Yummy!

Quick & Easy Pasta Fagioli

2 T olive oil
1 t butter
1 lb small shells
3 cans (14.5 oz) clear chicken broth
2 T crushed garlic...don't be a sissy, use more!
3 cans (14.5 oz) of either chick peas, white kidney beans or great northern beans...mix or match per taste...do NOT strain beans.

Cook shells. Brown garlic in oil & butter, add broth & beans to garlic and heat. Add the cooked shells and heat till serving temp.

You can top with grated cheese if desired or add clams or chicken if you wish.

Make sure you both eat this. As with all garlic dishes, not aromatic if only one eats this and is left with garlic breath!

World's Best Quick Lemonade

3 cups white grape juice
2.5 to 3 cups water
1 can (6 oz) frozen lemonade, thawed

Mix and serve over lots of ice.

No Mayo Chicken Salad

Blend in a blender:
1 raw egg
1 T Dijon mustard
1 t garlic powder
1 t lemon juice
1 Tb. olive oil
 Salt & Pepper to taste

Then add:
 1/2 red onion chopped
1 celery stalk chopped
4 ozs raisins (soaked in wine if possible)
2 T pine nuts

Mix all of the above to make dressing. Pour over cooked chicken and stir.

Crab, Cashew, Artichoke Dip

1 red bell pepper, chopped
3 green onions, sliced
2 fresh jalapeno peppers, diced
2 t olive oil
2 cans (6 oz each) lump crabmeat, drained and picked thru
1 can (14 oz) artichoke hearts, drained & chopped
1 cup mayo (low fat is okay)
1/2 cup grated parmesan cheese
1/2 cup cashews, halved

In a skillet, cook & stir pepper, green onions, and jalapenos in oil till tender. Mix crabmeat, artichokes, mayo & cheese; stir in to pepper mixture.

Put into 1 qt greased casserole dish and top with cashews. Bake at 375 for 25-30 minutes. Serve warm with crackers.

Holy Guacamole

Shred 1 head lettuce (easiest done in a food processor)
Mush 3-4 ripe large avocados
Chop 1 medium onion
Add I lemon juiced
Add 1 jar salsa (try Newman's own with peach, mango, or pineapple)
Add hot sauce or hot peppers to taste if desired.

Ay, Caramba, Lucy!

Julie's Orange Drink

6 oz frozen orange juice
1 cup milk
1 cup water
1/2 cup sugar
1 tsp. vanilla
10-12 ice cubes

Blend in a blender till smooth.

White Corn Chili

1 lb ground beef or ground turkey
1 15 oz can white corn or 1 lb frozen white corn
1 14 oz can diced tomatoes w/ garlic and onion
 2 cups salsa (Newman's Own with peach, pineapple, or mango)
1 16 oz can kidney beans, drained
 1 medium onion (1/2 used with meat, 1/2 as a topping)
1 tsp. garlic powder

Brown meat with 1/2 onion chopped. Drain & add remaining ingredients. Simmer 10 minutes.

OPTIONAL: You can add hot sauce to taste.

Top with shredded cheese, chopped scallions, chopped fresh tomato.

Best Alfredo Sauce

1/2 cup butter
5 cloves garlic, chopped
1 cup heavy cream
1 egg yolk
2 Tb. dried parsley
2 cups freshly grated Parmesan

In a large skillet, melt butter and add garlic. Cook on low for 5 minutes, stirring often. Be careful not to burn the garlic.

In a small bowl, add egg yolk to ¼ cup heavy cream, stir and put aside. Pour remaining cream into skillet, increase heat to medium high, mix rapidly with whisk as cream starts to boil. Slowly add egg/cream mixture, do NOT let egg curdle. Continue mixing until well blended. Add 1 cup Parmesan and continue whisking with cream. Pour in remaining Parmesan and add parsley.

Fruit Cocktail Tort

1 cup sugar
1 cup flour
1 tsp cinnamon
1 tsp baking soda

Mix together, then add:
 1 beaten egg
2 cups fruit cocktail w/juice (diet kind is OK).

Pour into greased 8x10 pan and top with:
½ cup brown sugar
¾ cup chopped nuts (optional)

Bake 1 hour @ 325 degrees

My Ukrainian Grandma's Kapusta

In a large sauce pan:
2 T olive oil
1 T butter
1 large onion, sliced
 2 T chopped garlic (or more to your taste)

Sauté the onion and garlic and then add:
1 head of sliced cabbage

Once the cabbage softens, add:
1 lb. can of sauerkraut (drained)

Simmer for 10 minutes, then add:
1 cup of chili sauce (Ketchup with seeds) or whatever kind of tomato product you prefer.

Mix, simmer 3 minutes, and serve. You may top it with rye or sesame seeds. Kielbasa can be served on the side or added during cooking.

 Note: This is an environmentally compatible dish as it produces copious amounts of methane gas.

Fish or Chicken Topping

1 chopped shallot
1 jar drained artichoke hearts
6 pieces of sun dried tomatoes in oil
3/4 cup heavy cream (or half & half)
1/4 cup sweet vermouth

Sauté shallot in small amount of oil from tomatoes. In a blender, chop shallots, artichoke hearts, and sun dried tomatoes. Return to pan. Add cream & vermouth and heat.

Serve over fish or chicken. Sprinkle with fresh basil.

Spicy Steak

Make the Rub:
1 1/2 T garlic powder
1 1/2 T basil
1 1/2 T oregano
1/2 t pepper
1/2 t salt

Use rib eye steaks cut 3/4 inch thick. Coat the steaks with rub. Pan fry in a tablespoon olive oil for 7 minutes each side; flip steaks only once.

Serve topped with lemon juice. Can also be topped with feta cheese or chopped black olives.

Easy Summer Salad

1/4 " slice of tomato
1/4 " slice of mozzarella
1 basil leaf
Small chunk of watermelon

Assemble in layers, starting with the tomato slice and topped by the watermelon on top.

Drizzle with Balsamic vinegar and salt.

Corn Mushroom Walnut Salad

1/2 lb. caramelized walnuts
    (I just fry them in butter and sugar)
1 lb. Portobello mushrooms, sautéed in butter
3 ears roasted husked corn

Assemble in layers, beginning with the caramelized walnuts, topped by mushrooms, and then corn.

Drizzle with Balsamic vinegar and salt.

Great Easy Recipes

<><><><><>

Do not hesitate to try a new recipe from the newspaper or magazine. Don't worry if you're a beginner in the kitchen. Your BB woman will be more than willing to help you along with some basic tips. She'll most likely share some of her favorite recipes too.

Remember to add in a little romance while cooking together. A hug and a smooch enhances the spice and flavor of any meal.

About the Author

Jay Ferry was born and reared in Norwich, Connecticut. He graduated from the prestigious Admiral Farragut Academy.

After a year of business studies at Syracuse University, he enlisted in the United States Navy. He was attached to Fighter Squadron 103 where he served aboard the aircraft carrier USS Saratoga and was deployed to the Mediterranean in 1968-69. Later he transferred to Attack Squadron 133 and served in Vietnam in 1970-71 aboard the aircraft carrier USS Ranger.

Upon completing his military duty, he obtained his Bachelor of Science degree from the University of Connecticut where he also lettered in basketball and baseball.

For most of his working career, Jay managed commercial properties, including high rise office buildings, shopping centers, malls, condos, and apartments. He holds the Certified Property Manager designation from the Institute of Real Estate Management.

As an entrepreneur, he founded and operated other businesses including Junior's Foods, Loretta's Hot Dogs, Ferry & Associates, Daytona Cobra, Monarch Management Group and Lease Review Services.

Jay's interests include many seasons coaching women's basketball. He also coached at two colleges and four high schools. He was the first non-minority women's basketball coach at Bethune Cookman University and holds that same distinction in the Mid-Eastern Athletic Conference.

He is a licensed FAA pilot. These days his main hobby is swing dancing. Jay is twice widowed and has one daughter and three grandchildren. He currently resides in Port Orange, Florida. This is his first book.

Jay can be contacted at: JayFerryauthor@yahoo.com.

Made in the USA
Columbia, SC
21 September 2020